Cycle Tours

Kent & East Sussex

Nick Cotton

Publisher: Cycle Tours is a joint venture between
CycleCity Guides and Cordee

CycleCity Guides
The Welsh Mill
Parkhill Drive
Frome
BA11 2LE
T: +44 (0)1373 453533

info@cyclecityguides.co.uk
www.cyclecityguides.co.uk

Cordee
11 Jacknell Road
Dodwells Bridge Industrial Estate
Hinckley
LE10 3BS
T: +44 (0)1455 611 185

charlie@cordee.co.uk
www.cordee.co.uk

ISBN: 978 1 904207 53 5

D0420090

Key to rides

1 On-road rides

1 Off-road rides

Quick reference chart

On-road rides

Ride number & title	Page	Distance	Grade
1	Wooded lanes north of Wrotham	8	32m (52km)	▲▲▲▲
2	A circuit of Sevenoaks from Wrotham	14	31m (50km)	▲▲▲▲
3	Southeast from Wrotham into the Medway Valley	20	30m (48km)	▲▲▲
4	Luddenham Marshes & the North Downs from Faversham	26	33m (53km)	▲▲
5	Labyrinths of lanes, south of Canterbury	32	34m (55km)	▲▲▲▲
6	Through the orchards of Kent, west of Sandwich	38	29m (47km)	▲
7	Sandwich, Deal & the Straits of Dover	44	31m (50km)	▲
8	Headcorn & the North Downs	50	36m (58km)	▲▲▲
9	Headcorn, Pluckley & Sissinghurst	56	28m (45km)	▲
10	West of Wye onto the North Downs	62	30m (48km)	▲▲▲
11	Labyrinths of lanes east of Wye	68	33m (53km)	▲▲▲▲▲
12	Hythe & Romney Marsh	74	26m (42km)	▲
13	Appledore & Romney Marsh	80	27m (43km)	▲
14	Burwash, Brightling & Mayfield	86	29m (47km)	▲▲▲▲
15	Battle, Bodiam, Beckley & Brede	92	33m (53km)	▲▲▲

Off-road rides

Ride number & title	Page	Distance	Grade
1	Ightham & Mereworth Woods	98	16m (26km)	▲▲▲
2	The North Downs Way from Charing to Hollingbourne	102	17m (27km)	▲
3	Wye, the Crundale Downs & King's Wood	106	16m (26km)	▲▲▲▲
4	Alfriston & Firle Beacon	110	11m (18km)	▲▲▲
5	Alfriston & Friston Forest	114	14m (23km)	▲▲▲▲▲

Grades

▲	Easy	
▲▲	Easy / Moderate	The grade is based on the amount of climbing
▲▲▲	Moderate	involved and, for off-road routes, the roughness
▲▲▲▲	Moderate / Strenuous	of the surface rather than the distance covered.
▲▲▲▲▲	Strenuous	

Kent & East Sussex

The geology of the area is dominated by three main features – the long chalk ridges of the North Downs and South Downs and, sandwiched between the two, the sandstone of the High Weald. The chalk downland offers the best mountain biking, especially along the top of the whaleback of hills running parallel with the South Coast that carries the South Downs Way from Winchester to Eastbourne. The South Downs Way has bridleway status along its entire length and makes a tough 2-3 day challenge.

By contrast the North Downs Way is a mixture of byways, bridleways and footpaths (on the latter you have no right to cycle) so rides here tend to link together short sections of byways and bridleways. These are rides that become more enjoyable with each outing as you come to recognise where the route goes without needing to refer to the map. Be warned that any ride on chalk and clay can get very muddy in the winter months or after heavy rain – these are definitely rides to enjoy after a few dry days in summer.

The region is not all hills; indeed, the rides across Romney Marsh are as easy as you will find anywhere. Similarly the lanes in the far east of Kent around Sandwich meander gently through a landscape of fruit orchards and offer easy options. The tougher challenges climb up onto the North Downs from Wrotham (near Maidstone), explore the High Weald around Sevenoaks or take you into the steep labyrinth of wooded lanes in the triangle formed by Canterbury, Dover and Ashford.

Kent and East Sussex are two of the most densely populated counties in England and also some of the wealthiest, with high levels of car ownership resulting in almost all the A and B roads being busy with traffic. The on-road rides try as much as possible to stay on the network of quieter lanes and avoid busy roads. With this in mind, the odd stretch of bridleway or byway (often part of the National Cycle Network) is occasionally used to offer direct crossings of A roads. Despite all this, you should be agreeably surprised by just how many miles of attractive quiet lanes still exist in the area.

Other useful information

Easy, traffic-free cycling for families and novices

Although the rides in this book are aimed at reasonably fit cyclists who are happy riding on the region's network of lanes or, in the case of mountain bikers, happy to ride on rough tracks, there may be times when your preference is for a ride that is also suitable for children or 'novice' cyclists. Listed below are some of the easier, flatter, traffic-free routes in the area.

Kent and East Sussex have several traffic-free paths on dismantled railways converted to recreational use, around reservoirs, or in Forestry Commission holdings.

Kent

1. Bewl Reservoir
13-mile ride around the largest reservoir in the Southeast:
www.bewl.co.uk
www.kent.gov.uk/leisureandculture/countrysideandcoast/cycling

2. Bedgebury Forest
2000 acre Forestry Commission holding with a 6-mile waymarked route aimed at families:
www.forestry.gov.uk/bedgebury
www.kent.gov.uk/leisureandculture/countrysideandcoast/cycling

3. Crab & Winkle Way from Canterbury to Whitstable
Railway path from Canterbury University north to the coast at Whitstable:
www.sustrans.org.uk

4. Tonbridge Castle to Penshurst Place
Cyclepath linking two historic buildings:
www.sustrans.org.uk

5. Margate to Reculver
Coastal promenade:
www.sustrans.org.uk

6. Hythe to Folkestone
Coastal promenade:
www.sustrans.org.uk

East Sussex

1. Friston Forest
Waymarked routes in woodland west of Eastbourne, accessed from the Visitor Centre at Exceat:
www.forestry.gov.uk and search **'Friston Forest Cycling'**

2. Cuckoo Trail
The most popular railway path in the Southeast, running 11 miles from Heathfield to Polegate (north of Eastbourne):
www.eastsussex.gov.uk and search **'Cuckoo Trail Map'**

3. Forest Way
Railway path running for 7 miles from East Grinstead to Groombridge:
www.eastsussex.gov.uk and search **'Forest Way Country Park'**

Cycle shops in the area
www.ikent.co.uk and search **'Cycling Shops'**
www.ieastsussex.co.uk and search **'Cycling Shops'**
www.thecyclepeople.com

Legend to 1:50,000 maps

Roads & paths

Motorway

Service area (S) · Junction number 1 · M 1 · Elevated

Primary route

Unfenced · Dual carriageway · A 470

Main road

Footbridge · A 493

Road under construction

Secondary road

B 4518

Narrow road with passing places

A 855 · B 885

Road generally more than 4m wide

Bridge

Road generally less than 4m wide

Other road

Path

Gradient: 1 in 5 and steeper. 1 in 7 to 1 in 5

Gates · Road tunnel

Passenger ferry · Vehicle ferry

Ferry P · Ferry V

Tourist information

⚔ 🚐	Camp site / caravan site
❋	Garden
⚑	Golf course or links
i *i*	Information centre, all year / seasonal
🦆	Nature reserve
P P&R P&R	Parking / Park & Ride, all year / seasonal
✕	Picnic site
	Selected place of tourist interest
☎	Public telephone
☎	Roadside assistance
☀	Viewpoint
V	Visitor centre
!	Walks / Trails
▲	Youth hostel
◉	World Heritage site / area
⊗	Recreation / leisure / sports centre

Railways

————	Track multiple or single
– – – –	Track under construction
┼─┼─┼─┼	Light rapid transit system, narrow gauge or tramway
	Bridge, footbridge
	Tunnel, cutting
● a	Station, (a) principal
————	Siding
┼─○─┼	Light rapid transit system station
LC	Level crossing
	Viaduct, embankment

Water features

Marsh or salting · Slopes · Cliff · High water mark

Towpath · Lock · Flat rock · Low water mark

Aqueduct · Canal · Ford · Lighthouse (in use)

Weir · Sand · Beacon

Lake · Footbridge · Bridge · Normal tidal limit · Dunes · Lighthouse (disused)

Shingle

Mud

Canal (dry)

4

General features

꠸꠸꠸꠸꠸ ꠸꠸꠸꠸꠸	Cutting, embankment
(dots)	Landfill site
(symbol)	Coniferous wood
(symbol)	Non-coniferous wood
(symbol)	Mixed wood
(symbol)	Orchard
(symbol)	Park or ornamental ground
(symbol)	Forestry Commission land
(symbol)	National Trust - always open
(symbol)	National Trust - limited access, observe local signs
(symbol)	National Trust for Scotland - always open
(symbol)	National Trust for Scotland - limited access, observe local signs
ʌ——ʌ——ʌ	Electricity transmission line (pylons shown at standard spacing)
> - -> - ->	Pipe line (arrow indicates direction of flow)
(symbol) ruin	Building
(symbol)	Important building (selected)
(symbol)	Bus or coach station
(symbol)	Glass structure
Ⓗ	Hospital
(symbol)	Place of worship with tower
(symbol)	Place of worship with spire, dome or minaret
+	Place of worship
(symbol)	Mast
(symbol)	Wind pump / wind turbine
(symbol)	Windmill with or without sails
+	Graticule intersection at 5' intervals

Rock features

Outcrop · Cliff · 650 · 600 · Scree

Public rights of way
(not applicable in Scotland)

·············	Footpath
—·—·—·—·—	Restricted byway
— — — — — —	Bridleway
-+-+-+-+-+-	Byway open to all traffic

Public rights of way shown have been taken from local authority definitive maps and later amendments. The symbols show the defined route so far as the scale of mapping will allow.

The representation on this map of any other road, track or path is no evidence of the existence of a right of way.

Other public access

· · · ·	Other route with public access
◆ ◆ ◆	National Trail, European Long Distance Path, Long Distance Route, selected Recreational Routes
● ● ●	On-road cycle route
○ ○ ○	Off-road cycle route
4	National Cycle Network Number
8	Regional Cycle Network Number
Danger Area	Firing and test ranges in the area Danger! Observe warning notices

Boundaries

+ — + — +	National
+ · + · + ·	District
—·—··—·—··	County, region or island area
(shaded)	National Park

Abbreviations

CH	Clubhouse
PH	Public house
PC	Public convenience (in rural area)
TH	Town Hall, Guildhall or equivalent
CG	Cattle grid
P	Post office
MP	Milepost
MS	Mile stone

Antiquities

+	Position of antiquity that cannot be drawn to scale
☆ ····	Visible earthwork
VILLA	Roman
Castle	Non-Roman
⚔	Battlefield (with date)

Heights

═══50═══	Contours are at 10 metre vertical intervals
·144	Heights are to the nearest metre above mean sea level
	Heights shown close to a triangulation pillar refer to the station height at ground level and not necessarily to the summit

5

Abbreviations and instructions

Instructions are given concisely to make them easy to follow while out riding. Remember to read one or two instructions ahead so that you do not miss a turning. This is most likely when you have to turn off a road / track you have been following for a while and are marked **Easy to miss** to warn you.

If there appears to be a contradiction between the instructions and what you actually see, always refer to the map. There are many reasons why, over the course of time, instructions may be subject to change with new roads, new junctions and new signposts.

Directions (all directions are given in bold)

L	left
R	right
SA	straight ahead
bear **L** or **R**	a turn which is less than 90 degrees (right-angle) at a fork in the road or on a sharp bend so that your course appears to be straight ahead; this is often written as 'in effect **SA**'
sharp **L** or **R**	a turn more acute than a right-angle
L or **R** sharply back on yourself	almost a U-turn
R then **L**	normally a T-junction where the next turn is visible from the first
R then first **L**	the second turning may be some distance from the first, ie '**R** then after ¹/₂ mile first **L**'

Junctions

T-j	T-junction, a junction where you have to give way
X-roads	crossroads, a junction where you may or may not have to give way
offset X-roads	the four roads are not in the form of a perfect cross and you will have to turn left then right, or vice versa, to continue the route

Signs

'Placename 2'	the words in quotation marks are those that appear on the signs, the numbers indicate the distance in miles unless stated otherwise
(NS)	not signposted

Instructions

An example of an easy instruction is:

4 At T-j at end of Smith Road by the White Swan Inn turn **R** on Brown Street 'Greentown 2, Redville 3'

There is more information in this instruction than you would normally need but things do change: pubs may close down and signs may be replaced, removed or vandalised.

An example of a difficult instruction is:

8 **Easy to miss:** shortly after the brow of the hill, on fast descent, first **R** (NS)

As you can see, there is no T-junction or 'Give Way' sign to halt you in your tracks, no signpost indicating where the right turn will take you and in addition you are picking up speed on a downhill, so you need to have your wits about you not to miss the turning.

Start
This is the suggested start point, coinciding with Instruction 1 on the map. There is no reason why you should not start at another point if it is more convenient.

Busy roads
These rides aim to keep to an absolute minimum time spent on busy roads but there are sometimes unavoidable sections where lane networks do not neatly link together. These busy roads are mentioned so that you are mentally prepared to deal with traffic, especially if there are children or less experienced cyclists in the group.

Off-road sections (on-road rides)
Occasionally a short distance on a traffic-free cyclepath, bridleway, byway or unclassified road can offer an alternative to a busy road. As the surfaces are not sealed you may encounter puddles or muddy water, especially in winter or after prolonged rain.

Terrain
This brief description of the terrain covered by the route should be read in conjunction with the cross-profile diagram at the foot of the page to help you plan your journey.

Distance
The distance (shown in miles and kilometres) is, of course, that from the beginning to the end of the ride. However, if you wish to shorten the ride because of tiredness, mechanical problems, a change in the weather or simply lack of time then the maps enable you to do so.

Grade
There are five grades of difficulty:
Easy
Easy / Moderate
Moderate
Moderate / Strenuous
Strenuous
The grade is based on the amount of climbing involved and, for off-road routes, the roughness of the surface rather than the distance covered.

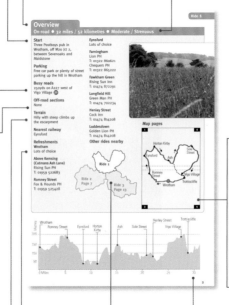

Map pages
Route overviews show how the maps have been laid out on the pages. Page numbers are shown in the corners. The diagrams show start points, route direction and some of the villages on or near the route.

Other rides nearby
Schematic map showing where nearby rides overlap. Shorter or longer rides can be created by mixing and matching rides.

Cross-profile
Shows heights in metres and distance travelled. Places along the route are shown.

Refreshments
More than three pubs or a mixture of pubs, cafés and tearooms in any one place is indicated by 'Lots of choice'. Otherwise, names of pubs, cafés and tearooms are listed, where possible with telephone numbers so that you can call ahead to check on opening times and when food is served.

Wooded lanes north of Wrotham

The village of Wrotham, nestling beneath the North Downs escarpment halfway between Maidstone and Sevenoaks, is a fine base for exploring the area by bike whether on-road or off-road. It has several pubs, free parking, is easily accessed by car from the M20 / M26 or by train with nearby stations at Kemsing and Borough Green. This ride explores the extraordinary network of lanes on the hilly, wooded North Downs lying to the north of Wrotham between the River Darent and the River Medway. The ride starts with a steep climb taking you directly to the highest point of the ride at 690ft (210m) by the masts near Romney Street. On a clear day there are views across southeast London to the towers of Canary Wharf. The descent to Eynsford seems to go on forever and you may wish to stop to appreciate some of the best views of the day. From Eynsford there is the chance of a cultural diversion to visit

the splendours of Lullingstone Castle and Lullingstone Roman Villa, both less than a mile off the route. Cross the River Darent, pass through the pretty village of Farningham and climb back up on the North Downs, navigating your way eastwards through

the maze of lanes that avoid the built-up areas and busy roads to arrive at the tiny village of Luddesdown. The longest climb of the day takes you south to Vigo Village. A somewhat circuitous route to avoid the busy A227 leads via Trottiscliffe back to the start.

Overview

On-road ● **32 miles / 52 kilometres** ● **Moderate / Strenuous**

Start
Three Postboys pub in Wrotham, off M20 Jct 2, between Sevenoaks and Maidstone

Parking
Free car park or plenty of street parking up the hill in Wrotham

Busy roads
250yds on A227 west of Vigo Village **25**

Off-road sections
None

Terrain
Hilly with steep climbs up the escarpment

Nearest railway
Eynsford

Refreshments
Wrotham
Lots of choice

Above Kemsing (Cotmans Ash Lane)
Rising Sun PH
T: 01959 522683

Romney Street
Fox & Hounds PH
T: 01959 525428

Eynsford
Lots of choice

Farningham
Lion PH
T: 01322 860621
Chequers PH
T: 01322 865222

Fawkham Green
Rising Sun Inn
T: 01474 872291

Longfield Hill
Green Man PH
T: 01474 702234

Henley Street
Cock Inn
T: 01474 814208

Luddesdown
Golden Lion PH
T: 01474 814208

Other rides nearby

Map pages

Ride 1

Ride 2
Page 14

Ride 3
Page 20

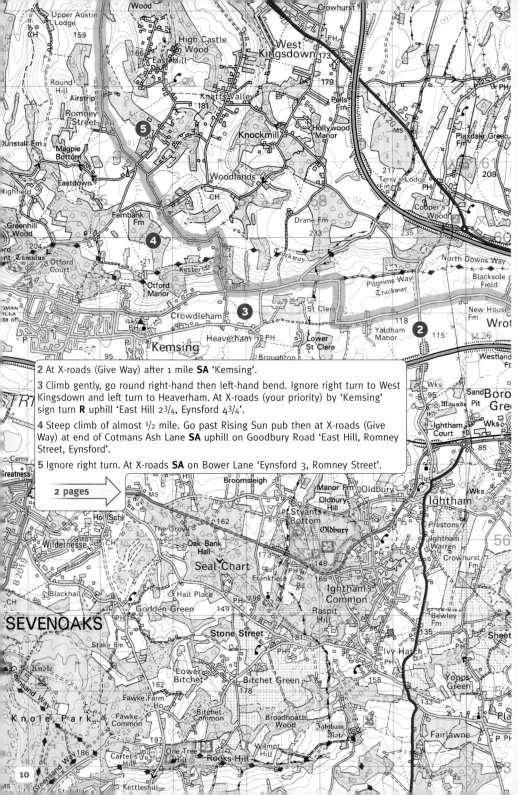

2 At X-roads (Give Way) after 1 mile **SA** 'Kemsing'.

3 Climb gently, go round right-hand then left-hand bend. Ignore right turn to West Kingsdown and left turn to Heaverham. At X-roads (your priority) by 'Kemsing' sign turn **R** uphill 'East Hill 2¾, Eynsford 4¾'.

4 Steep climb of almost ½ mile. Go past Rising Sun pub then at X-roads (Give Way) at end of Cotmans Ash Lane **SA** uphill on Goodbury Road 'East Hill, Romney Street, Eynsford'.

5 Ignore right turn. At X-roads **SA** on Bower Lane 'Eynsford 3, Romney Street'.

2 pages ➡

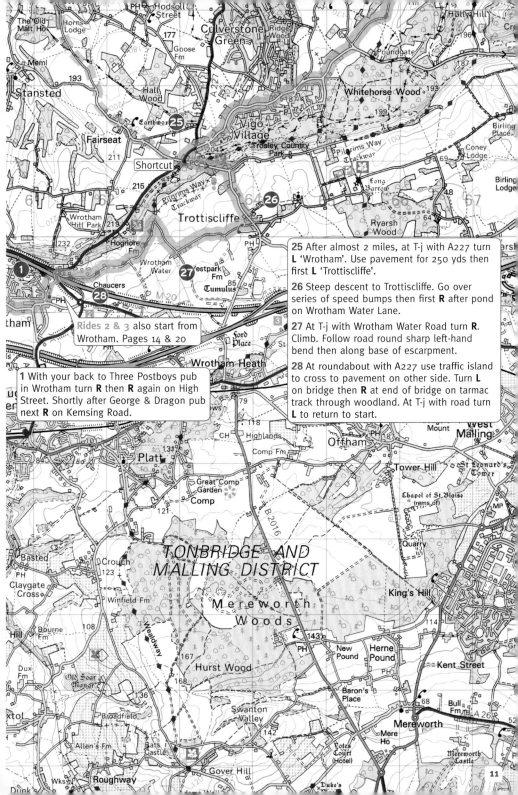

25 After almost 2 miles, at T-j with A227 turn **L** 'Wrotham'. Use pavement for 250 yds then first **L** 'Trottiscliffe'.

26 Steep descent to Trottiscliffe. Go over series of speed bumps then first **R** after pond on Wrotham Water Lane.

27 At T-j with Wrotham Water Road turn **R**. Climb. Follow road round sharp left-hand bend then along base of escarpment.

28 At roundabout with A227 use traffic island to cross to pavement on other side. Turn **L** on bridge then **R** at end of bridge on tarmac track through woodland. At T-j with road turn **L** to return to start.

Rides **2 & 3** also start from Wrotham. Pages 14 & 20

1 With your back to Three Postboys pub in Wrotham turn **R** then **R** again on High Street. Shortly after George & Dragon pub next **R** on Kemsing Road.

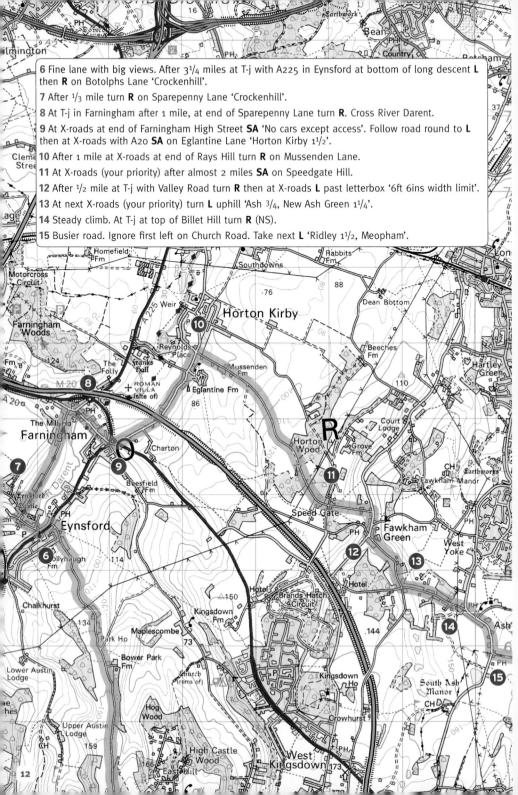

6 Fine lane with big views. After 3¹/₄ miles at T-j with A225 in Eynsford at bottom of long descent **L** then **R** on Botolphs Lane 'Crockenhill'.

7 After ¹/₃ mile turn **R** on Sparepenny Lane 'Crockenhill'.

8 At T-j in Farningham after 1 mile, at end of Sparepenny Lane turn **R**. Cross River Darent.

9 At X-roads at end of Farningham High Street **SA** 'No cars except access'. Follow road round to **L** then at X-roads with A20 **SA** on Eglantine Lane 'Horton Kirby 1¹/₂'.

10 After 1 mile at X-roads at end of Rays Hill turn **R** on Mussenden Lane.

11 At X-roads (your priority) after almost 2 miles **SA** on Speedgate Hill.

12 After ¹/₂ mile at T-j with Valley Road turn **R** then at X-roads **L** past letterbox '6ft 6ins width limit'.

13 At next X-roads (your priority) turn **L** uphill 'Ash ³/₄, New Ash Green 1¹/₄'.

14 Steady climb. At T-j at top of Billet Hill turn **R** (NS).

15 Busier road. Ignore first left on Church Road. Take next **L** 'Ridley 1¹/₂, Meopham'.

16 Descend, ignore two closely spaced right turns then shortly next **L** on Hartley Bottom Road 'Longfield Hill'.

17 After just over 1 mile at T-j turn **R** 'Longfield Hill 2'.

18 Ignore one right and two left turns over next 1½ miles. Immediately before blue and white width limit sign take next **R** (NS).

19 At T-j with B260 at end of Manor Road by Green Man pub turn **L** then first **R** (NS).

20 Descend then climb. At X-roads with A227 **SA** on Nurstead Church Lane 'St Mildred's Church'.

21 Ignore left turn. At T-j at end of White Post Lane turn **R**. Shortly, at end of Round Street turn **R** again 'Sole Street, Meopham' then first **L** 'Luddesdown, Gold Street'.

22 Go past Cock Inn then at T-j by Golden Lion pub at end of Henley Street turn **L** 'Cuxton' then **R** 'Great Buckland 1¾'. At T-j by telegraph pole at top of climb bear **R** (NS).

23 After 1 mile, at fork with 'No through road' sign to left, bear **R** on lower road. Climb steeply then at junction at top by 3-way sign turn **L** 'Harvel'.

24 At X-roads / T-j at end of Leywood Road turn **R** 'Vigo, Trosley Country Park'.

2 pages

A circuit of Sevenoaks from Wrotham

As indicated in the previous ride, Wrotham is one of those unsung places that is a perfect cycling base with networks of quiet lanes radiating off in all directions. As it is also on the North Downs Way, it offers good mountain biking on the broad chalk tracks that criss-cross the escarpment. This ride explores the countryside to the west and southwest of Wrotham, describing a circuit around Sevenoaks. The first half of the ride is a real rollercoaster, climbing steeply up onto the North Downs on narrow, thickly wooded lanes, dropping down into the Darent Valley, climbing to Knockholt, descending to Brasted (where there is an excellent café), then the final big climb of the day up to The Chart and Ide Hill. Just before Ide Hill you may wish to visit Emmetts Garden, a National Trust property famous for its rare and exotic trees and shrubs (especially noted for their autumn colour) with dramatic views from the hilltop location and an open-air tearoom. For more details go to www.nationaltrust.org.uk. The southern half of the ride is less hilly as you gradually lose height from the masts on River Hill to the south of Sevenoaks down to the beautiful timbered buildings of Ightham. A second worthwhile detour is to Ightham Mote, a perfect medieval moated manor house set in a secluded valley. The hall was built in the 14th century. The stonework in the courtyard forms a Tudor rose. For more details go to the National Trust website mentioned above.

Overview

On-road ● 33 miles / 51 kilometres ● Moderate / Strenuous

Start
Three Postboys pub in Wrotham, off M20 Jct 2, between Sevenoaks and Maidstone

Parking
Free car park or plenty of street parking up the hill in Wrotham

Busy roads
● A225 east of Shoreham (pavement) **7** to **8**

● A25 in Brasted (30 mph speed limit) **15**

● A225 south of Sevenoaks (pavement) **22**

Off-road sections
None

Terrain
Hilly in the first half of the ride, climbing three times up and down the North Downs escarpment and the High Weald

Nearest railway
Shoreham or Knockholt

Refreshments
Wrotham
Lots of choice

North of Kemsing (top of North Downs)
Rising Sun PH
T: 01959 522683

Shoreham
Lots of choice

Halstead
Rose & Crown PH
T: 01959 533120

Brasted
White Hart PH
T: 01959 560651

Ide Hill
Cock Inn
T: 01732 750310

Stone Street
Snail PH
T: 01732 810233

Ightham
Chequers PH
T: 01732 882396

Map pages

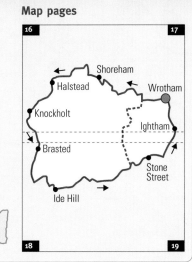

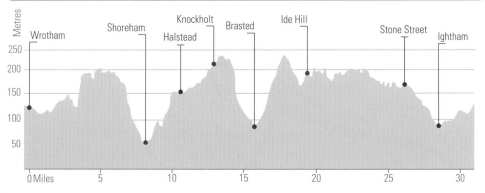

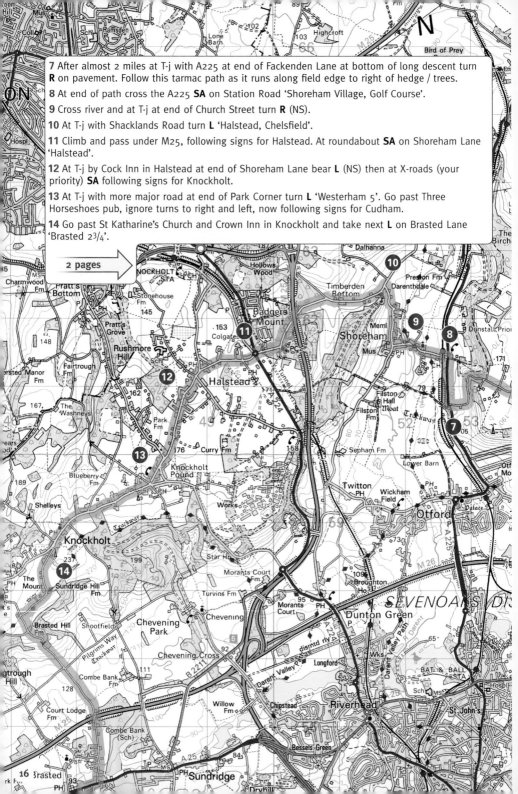

7 After almost 2 miles at T-j with A225 at end of Fackenden Lane at bottom of long descent turn **R** on pavement. Follow this tarmac path as it runs along field edge to right of hedge / trees.

8 At end of path cross the A225 **SA** on Station Road 'Shoreham Village, Golf Course'.

9 Cross river and at T-j at end of Church Street turn **R** (NS).

10 At T-j with Shacklands Road turn **L** 'Halstead, Chelsfield'.

11 Climb and pass under M25, following signs for Halstead. At roundabout **SA** on Shoreham Lane 'Halstead'.

12 At T-j by Cock Inn in Halstead at end of Shoreham Lane bear **L** (NS) then at X-roads (your priority) **SA** following signs for Knockholt.

13 At T-j with more major road at end of Park Corner turn **L** 'Westerham 5'. Go past Three Horseshoes pub, ignore turns to right and left, now following signs for Cudham.

14 Go past St Katharine's Church and Crown Inn in Knockholt and take next **L** on Brasted Lane 'Brasted 2¾'.

2 pages ➡

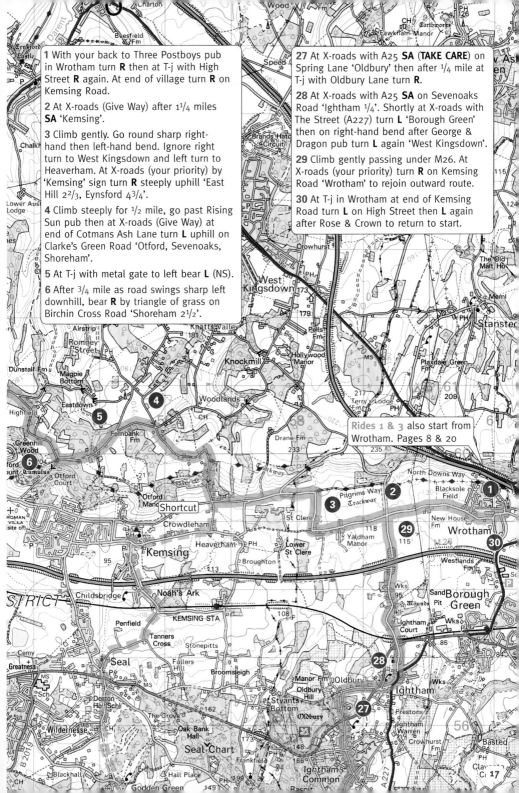

1 With your back to Three Postboys pub in Wrotham turn **R** then at T-j with High Street **R** again. At end of village turn **R** on Kemsing Road.

2 At X-roads (Give Way) after 1¼ miles **SA** 'Kemsing'.

3 Climb gently. Go round sharp right-hand then left-hand bend. Ignore right turn to West Kingsdown and left turn to Heaverham. At X-roads (your priority) by 'Kemsing' sign turn **R** steeply uphill 'East Hill 2⅔, Eynsford 4¾'.

4 Climb steeply for ½ mile, go past Rising Sun pub then at X-roads (Give Way) at end of Cotmans Ash Lane turn **L** uphill on Clarke's Green Road 'Otford, Sevenoaks, Shoreham'.

5 At T-j with metal gate to left bear **L** (NS).

6 After ¾ mile as road swings sharp left downhill, bear **R** by triangle of grass on Birchin Cross Road 'Shoreham 2½'.

27 At X-roads with A25 **SA** (**TAKE CARE**) on Spring Lane 'Oldbury' then after ¼ mile at T-j with Oldbury Lane turn **R**.

28 At X-roads with A25 **SA** on Sevenoaks Road 'Ightham ¼'. Shortly at X-roads with The Street (A227) turn **L** 'Borough Green' then on right-hand bend after George & Dragon pub turn **L** again 'West Kingsdown'.

29 Climb gently passing under M26. At X-roads (your priority) turn **R** on Kemsing Road 'Wrotham' to rejoin outward route.

30 At T-j in Wrotham at end of Kemsing Road turn **L** on High Street then **L** again after Rose & Crown to return to start.

Rides 1 & 3 also start from Wrotham. Pages 8 & 20

17

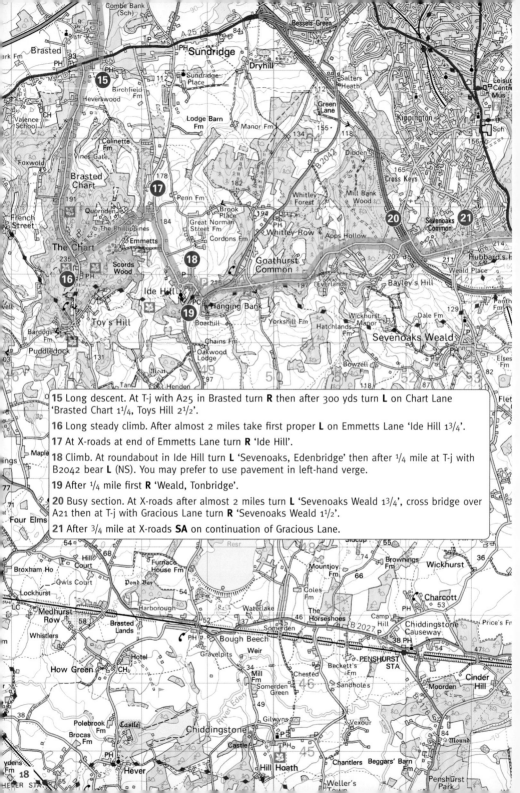

15 Long descent. At T-j with A25 in Brasted turn **R** then after 300 yds turn **L** on Chart Lane 'Brasted Chart 1¼, Toys Hill 2½'.

16 Long steady climb. After almost 2 miles take first proper **L** on Emmetts Lane 'Ide Hill 1¾'.

17 At X-roads at end of Emmetts Lane turn **R** 'Ide Hill'.

18 Climb. At roundabout in Ide Hill turn **L** 'Sevenoaks, Edenbridge' then after ¼ mile at T-j with B2042 bear **L** (NS). You may prefer to use pavement in left-hand verge.

19 After ¼ mile first **R** 'Weald, Tonbridge'.

20 Busy section. At X-roads after almost 2 miles turn **L** 'Sevenoaks Weald 1¾', cross bridge over A21 then at T-j with Gracious Lane turn **R** 'Sevenoaks Weald 1½'.

21 After ¾ mile at X-roads **SA** on continuation of Gracious Lane.

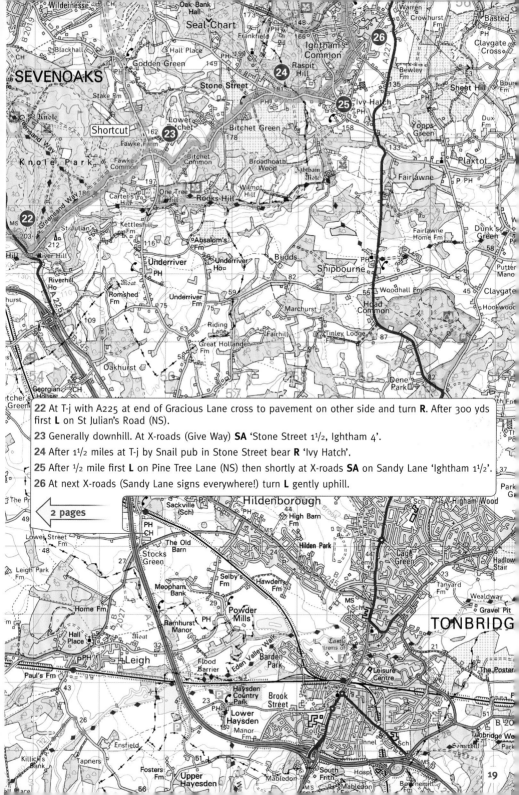

22 At T-j with A225 at end of Gracious Lane cross to pavement on other side and turn **R**. After 300 yds first **L** on St Julian's Road (NS).

23 Generally downhill. At X-roads (Give Way) **SA** 'Stone Street 1½, Ightham 4'.

24 After 1½ miles at T-j by Snail pub in Stone Street bear **R** 'Ivy Hatch'.

25 After ½ mile first **L** on Pine Tree Lane (NS) then shortly at X-roads **SA** on Sandy Lane 'Ightham 1½'.

26 At next X-roads (Sandy Lane signs everywhere!) turn **L** gently uphill.

← 2 pages

Southeast from Wrotham into the Medway Valley

The Medway Valley is explored in this ride, the River Medway being Kent's principal river, its source in the High Weald to the south of Crawley and its mouth on the north Kent coast at Rochester and Chatham. Starting from Wrotham, nestling under the steep chalk escarpment of the North Downs, the route meanders and undulates through the attractive villages of Trottiscliffe and Addington to arrive at the myriad fine buildings in West Malling. St Leonard's Tower is an impressive Norman keep, built by Bishop Gundulf in the 11th century. He also built the White Tower in the Tower of London and the castles of Rochester and Colchester. Grotesque faces adorn the tombstones at the Norman Church of St Mary. The High Street dates mainly from the Georgian era. After leaving West Malling you cross fruit orchards and drop down to cross the River Medway between East Barming and Kettle Corner on a bridge now shut to vehicles. The longest and steepest climb of the day takes you south on a lane gradually falling into benign neglect. Busier roads are joined near Yalding where two long stone medieval bridges lead into the wide curving street of mellow brick and timber houses where two main tributaries, the Teise and the Beult, flow into the River Medway. Yalding lies in the heart of Kent's hop-farming country. North and west from here you rejoin the network of quiet lanes that lead through more orchards and quintessential Kentish scenery back to Wrotham.

Overview

On-road ● 30 miles / 48 kilometres ● Moderate

Start
Three Postboys pub, Wrotham, off M20 Jct 2, between Sevenoaks and Maidstone

Parking
Free car park or plenty of street parking up the hill in Wrotham

Busy roads
● 2 miles on B2010 / B2162 through Yalding **18**

● 200yds on A228 in Hadlow **22**

● 500yds on A227 in Ightham **27**

Off-road sections
Short section on wide gravel track south of Farleigh Green **14**

Terrain
Undulating with several climbs of 100-200ft (30-60m) and two longer ones

Nearest railway
West Malling or Yalding

Refreshments
Wrotham
Lots of choice

Trottiscliffe
Plough Inn
T: 01732 822233

Addington
Angel Inn
T: 01732 842117

West Malling
Lots of choice

East Malling Heath
North Pole PH
T: 01622 812392

East Barming
Bull PH
T: 01622 726468

Farleigh Green
Good Intent PH
T: 01622 812426

Yalding
Walnut Tree PH
T: 01622 814266

Plaxtol
Golding Hop PH
T: 01732 882150

Other rides nearby

Map pages

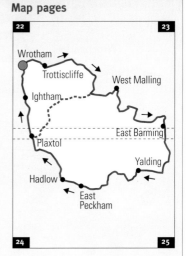

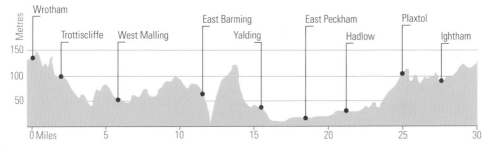

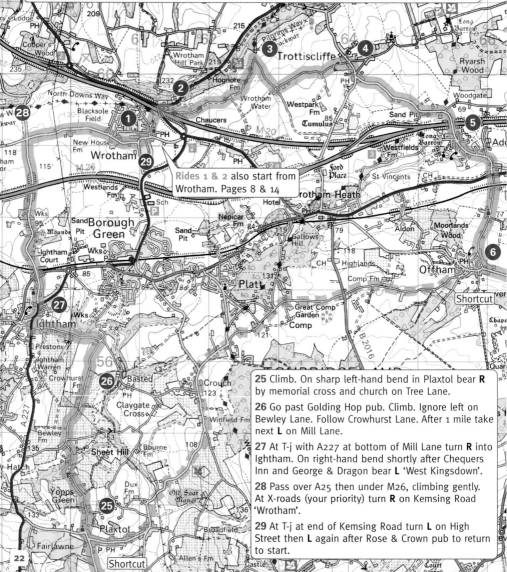

1 With your back to Three Postboys pub in Wrotham turn **L** uphill. At fork bear **R** on no through road. Just before lay-by with recycling bins and 'No entry' sign turn **R** on narrow tarmac path.

2 At T-j with busy road turn **L** on pavement across bridge then just before roundabout use traffic island to cross on to minor lane opposite 'North Downs Way'.

3 Ignore right turn on Nepicar Lane. Follow road downhill round sharp right-hand bend. **Easy to miss:** on fast descent take first **L** (NS) immediately before first house (made of timber and brick).

4 At X-roads at end of Wrotham Water Lane turn **R** downhill. Go **SA** through Trottiscliffe 'Addington 1¼, West Malling 3'.

5 Cross bridge over M20. Go past Angel Inn in Addington. At X-roads with A20 **SA** on Church Road 'Offham 1'.

6 At T-j with Teston Road in Offham turn **L** (NS). **Easy to miss:** after ½ mile of descent, take second of two closely spaced **L** turns on Offham Road.

Rides 1 & 2 also start from Wrotham. Pages 8 & 14

25 Climb. On sharp left-hand bend in Plaxtol bear **R** by memorial cross and church on Tree Lane.

26 Go past Golding Hop pub. Climb. Ignore left on Bewley Lane. Follow Crowhurst Lane. After 1 mile take next **L** on Mill Lane.

27 At T-j with A227 at bottom of Mill Lane turn **R** into Ightham. On right-hand bend shortly after Chequers Inn and George & Dragon bear **L** 'West Kingsdown'.

28 Pass over A25 then under M26, climbing gently. At X-roads (your priority) turn **R** on Kemsing Road 'Wrotham'.

29 At T-j at end of Kemsing Road turn **L** on High Street then **L** again after Rose & Crown pub to return to start.

Shortcut

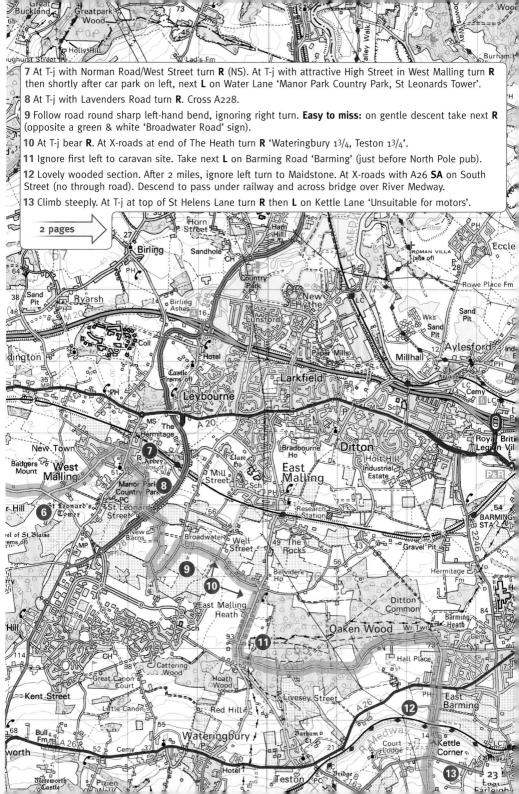

7 At T-j with Norman Road/West Street turn **R** (NS). At T-j with attractive High Street in West Malling turn **R** then shortly after car park on left, next **L** on Water Lane 'Manor Park Country Park, St Leonards Tower'.

8 At T-j with Lavenders Road turn **R**. Cross A228.

9 Follow road round sharp left-hand bend, ignoring right turn. **Easy to miss:** on gentle descent take next **R** (opposite a green & white 'Broadwater Road' sign).

10 At T-j bear **R**. At X-roads at end of The Heath turn **R** 'Wateringbury 1³/₄, Teston 1³/₄'.

11 Ignore first left to caravan site. Take next **L** on Barming Road 'Barming' (just before North Pole pub).

12 Lovely wooded section. After 2 miles, ignore left turn to Maidstone. At X-roads with A26 **SA** on South Street (no through road). Descend to pass under railway and across bridge over River Medway.

13 Climb steeply. At T-j at top of St Helens Lane turn **R** then **L** on Kettle Lane 'Unsuitable for motors'.

2 pages →

22 Ignore left and right turns for 2 miles. At T-j with A26 in Hadlow at end of Court Lane turn **L** then after 250 yds **R** on Carpenters Lane 'Shipbourne 2¾, Plaxtol 3'.

23 At T-j by triangle of grass with trees in it turn **L** 'Plaxtol, Shipbourne'.

24 Go **SA** at X-roads, ignore right turn, go **SA** at second X-roads then take next **R** on School Lane 'Plaxtol' by red-brick and timber house.

2 pages

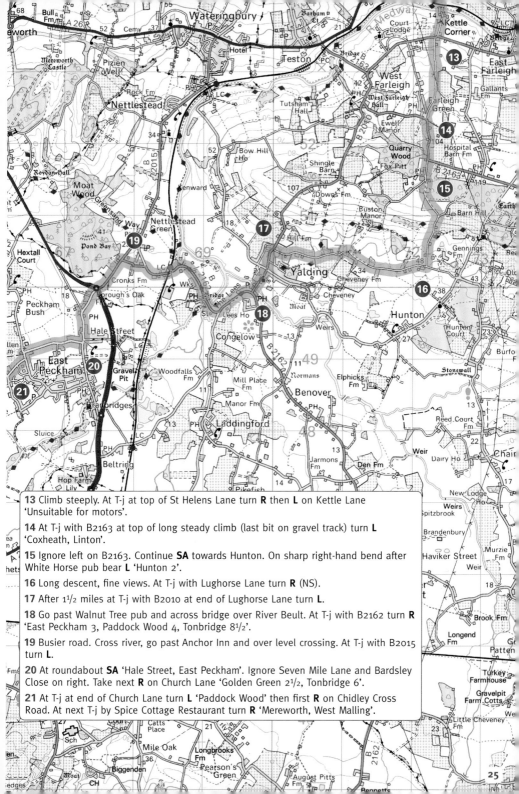

13 Climb steeply. At T-j at top of St Helens Lane turn **R** then **L** on Kettle Lane 'Unsuitable for motors'.

14 At T-j with B2163 at top of long steady climb (last bit on gravel track) turn **L** 'Coxheath, Linton'.

15 Ignore left on B2163. Continue **SA** towards Hunton. On sharp right-hand bend after White Horse pub bear **L** 'Hunton 2'.

16 Long descent, fine views. At T-j with Lughorse Lane turn **R** (NS).

17 After 1½ miles at T-j with B2010 at end of Lughorse Lane turn **L**.

18 Go past Walnut Tree pub and across bridge over River Beult. At T-j with B2162 turn **R** 'East Peckham 3, Paddock Wood 4, Tonbridge 8½'.

19 Busier road. Cross river, go past Anchor Inn and over level crossing. At T-j with B2015 turn **L**.

20 At roundabout **SA** 'Hale Street, East Peckham'. Ignore Seven Mile Lane and Bardsley Close on right. Take next **R** on Church Lane 'Golden Green 2½, Tonbridge 6'.

21 At T-j at end of Church Lane turn **L** 'Paddock Wood' then first **R** on Chidley Cross Road. At next T-j by Spice Cottage Restaurant turn **R** 'Mereworth, West Malling'.

Luddenham Marshes & the North Downs from Faversham

Faversham is an attractive port and market town full of listed buildings where pilgrims would stop on their way to Canterbury. Wooden pillars support the 16th century Guildhall and covered market. Northwest of Faversham the ride offers a sense of remoteness as you cross Luddenham Marshes, looking across The Swale towards the Isle of Sheppey, a remoteness that belies your proximity to motorways, railways and the densely populated towns of the southeast. National

Cycle Network Route 1 (NCN 1) is followed west from the start on a mixture of lanes and gravel tracks past orchards and polytunnels full of soft fruit to the marina at Conyer, a rather incongruous collection of brightly coloured yachts and sailing craft in this highly productive agricultural area. Leave NCN 1 and turn south through the maze of lanes weaving between more orchards of apples and pears through the pretty village of Lynsted. Chilham is the next highlight with its Jacobean mansion, Norman castle,

timbered buildings, pubs and tearooms. After wiggling your way north through to Boughton Street, rejoin NCN 1 for a traffic-free approach back into the heart of Faversham.

NB In this part of Kent there is an amazingly dense lane network with lots of junctions: this is definitely a ride that is better second and third time round when you know where you are going and don't need to keep consulting the instructions.

Overview

On-road ● 33 miles / 53 kilometres ● Easy / Moderate

Start
Market Hall in the centre of Faversham, off the M2 west of Canterbury

Parking
Several Pay & Display car parks in Faversham

Busy roads
300yds on A2 east of Bapchild (use pavement) **8**

Off-road sections
● Gravel path (National Cycle Network Route 1) west of Conyer around Conyer Creek **5** to **6**

● Gravel path (National Cycle Network Route 1) east of Faversham to return to the start **27** to **28**

Terrain
The northern half of the ride is pretty flat, the southern half is undulating. Three noticeable climbs

Nearest railway
Faversham

Refreshments
Faversham
Lots of choice

Conyer Quay
Ship Inn
T: 01795 520778

Lynsted
Black Lion PH
T: 01795 521229

Chilham
Lots of choice

Old Wives Lees
Star Inn
T: 01227 730213

Boughton Street
White Horse PH
T: 01227 751343

Graveney
Four Horseshoes PH
T: 01795 532095

Thruxton
White Horse PH
T: 01267 772401

Other rides nearby

Map pages

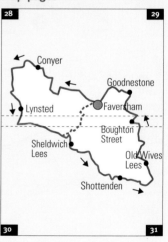

3 Ignore right on Bunting Close and take next **R** on Tin Shop Hill. At X-roads at end of Tin Shop Hill **SA** 'Oare ¹/₂, Harty Ferry 2'. Shortly, with 'No through road' sign ahead, turn **L** 'Sittingbourne, National Cycle Network Route 1' (shown from now on as 'NCN 1').

4 After 1¹/₂ miles at T-j by level crossing turn **R** 'Teynham 2, Sittingbourne 5' then after ¹/₂ mile, at end of row of modern red-brick houses on right, next **R** 'NCN 1' to pass under railway bridge.

5 At T-j after 1 mile turn **R** 'NCN 1, Conyer ³/₄'. After ¹/₂ mile at end of road, with 'The Quay' (no through road) to right, go **SA** on broad track 'Swale Marina'.

6 Follow NCN 1 signs, turning **L** just before marina onto rougher track. Follow gravel path around edge of marina then away from it. Rejoin tarmac and turn **L** 'Sittingbourne, NCN 1'.

7 At T-j bear **L** downhill, leaving NCN 1 (which goes right uphill).

8 Ignore right turn. Go under railway bridge and ignore left turn. At T-j with A2 turn **L** 'Faversham'. Use pavement for 300 yds then turn first **R** 'Dully'.

9 Easy to miss: after almost 1 mile turn first **L** (NS).

10 At T-j turn **R** 'Lynsted ¹/₃, Doddington 3' then after ¹/₃ mile at next T-j turn **R** again 'Doddington 2³/₄, Newnham 4¹/₂, Lengham 7³/₄'. Go through Lynsted.

11 After 1¹/₄ miles as road swings sharp right, bear **L** soon running parallel with M2. At fork of roads after ³/₄ mile bear **R** 'Newnham'.

2 pages →

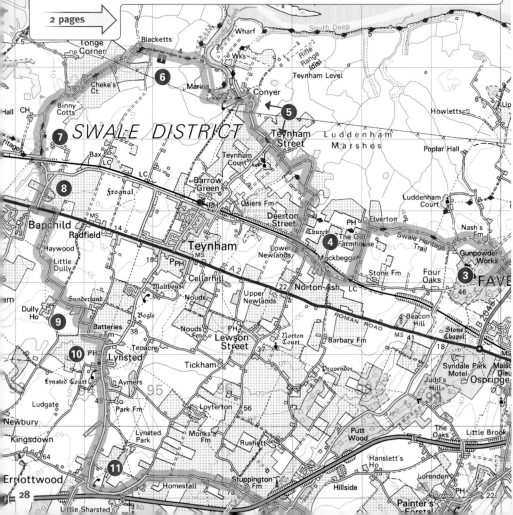

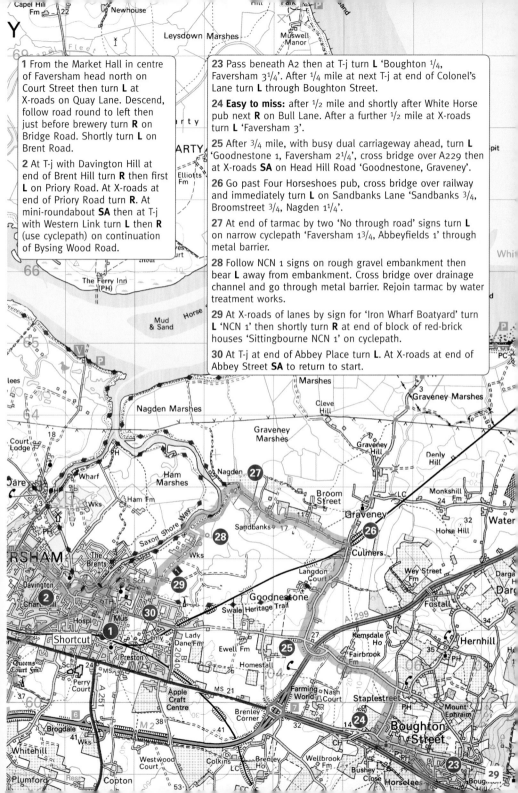

1 From the Market Hall in centre of Faversham head north on Court Street then turn **L** at X-roads on Quay Lane. Descend, follow road round to left then just before brewery turn **R** on Bridge Road. Shortly turn **L** on Brent Road.

2 At T-j with Davington Hill at end of Brent Hill turn **R** then first **L** on Priory Road. At X-roads at end of Priory Road turn **R**. At mini-roundabout **SA** then at T-j with Western Link turn **L** then **R** (use cyclepath) on continuation of Bysing Wood Road.

23 Pass beneath A2 then at T-j turn **L** 'Boughton 1/4, Faversham 31/4'. After 1/4 mile at next T-j at end of Colonel's Lane turn **L** through Boughton Street.

24 Easy to miss: after 1/2 mile and shortly after White Horse pub next **R** on Bull Lane. After a further 1/2 mile at X-roads turn **L** 'Faversham 3'.

25 After 3/4 mile, with busy dual carriageway ahead, turn **L** 'Goodnestone 1, Faversham 21/4', cross bridge over A229 then at X-roads **SA** on Head Hill Road 'Goodnestone, Graveney'.

26 Go past Four Horseshoes pub, cross bridge over railway and immediately turn **L** on Sandbanks Lane 'Sandbanks 3/4, Broomstreet 3/4, Nagden 11/4'.

27 At end of tarmac by two 'No through road' signs turn **L** on narrow cyclepath 'Faversham 13/4, Abbeyfields 1' through metal barrier.

28 Follow NCN 1 signs on rough gravel embankment then bear **L** away from embankment. Cross bridge over drainage channel and go through metal barrier. Rejoin tarmac by water treatment works.

29 At X-roads of lanes by sign for 'Iron Wharf Boatyard' turn **L** 'NCN 1' then shortly turn **R** at end of block of red-brick houses 'Sittingbourne NCN 1' on cyclepath.

30 At T-j at end of Abbey Place turn **L**. At X-roads at end of Abbey Street **SA** to return to start.

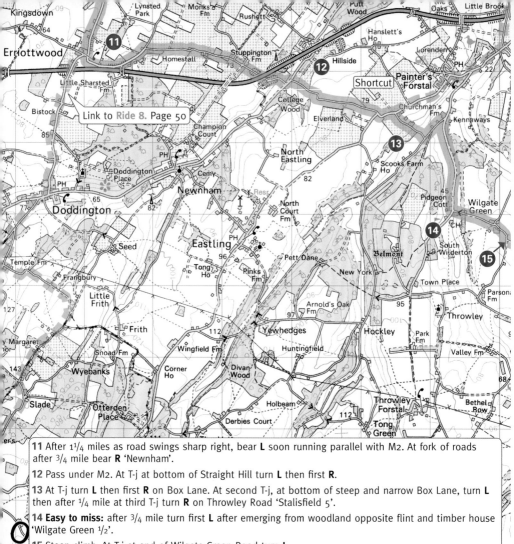

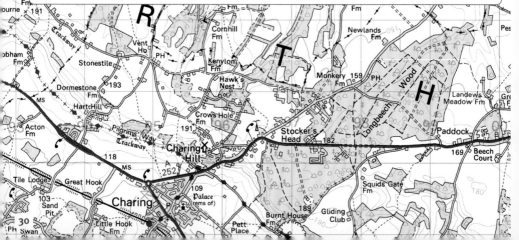

11 After 1¼ miles as road swings sharp right, bear **L** soon running parallel with M2. At fork of roads after ¾ mile bear **R** 'Newnham'.

12 Pass under M2. At T-j at bottom of Straight Hill turn **L** then first **R**.

13 At T-j turn **L** then first **R** on Box Lane. At second T-j, at bottom of steep and narrow Box Lane, turn **L** then after ¼ mile at third T-j turn **R** on Throwley Road 'Stalisfield 5'.

14 **Easy to miss:** after ¾ mile turn first **L** after emerging from woodland opposite flint and timber house 'Wilgate Green ½'.

15 Steep climb. At T-j at end of Wilgate Green Road turn **L**.

Link to **Ride 8**. Page 50

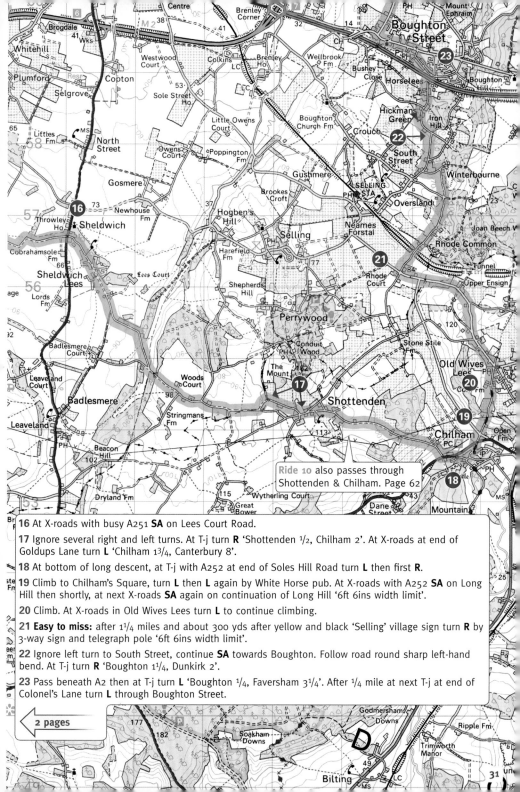

16 At X-roads with busy A251 **SA** on Lees Court Road.

17 Ignore several right and left turns. At T-j turn **R** 'Shottenden ½, Chilham 2'. At X-roads at end of Goldups Lane turn **L** 'Chilham 1¾, Canterbury 8'.

18 At bottom of long descent, at T-j with A252 at end of Soles Hill Road turn **L** then first **R**.

19 Climb to Chilham's Square, turn **L** then **L** again by White Horse pub. At X-roads with A252 **SA** on Long Hill then shortly, at next X-roads **SA** again on continuation of Long Hill '6ft 6ins width limit'.

20 Climb. At X-roads in Old Wives Lees turn **L** to continue climbing.

21 **Easy to miss:** after 1¼ miles and about 300 yds after yellow and black 'Selling' village sign turn **R** by 3-way sign and telegraph pole '6ft 6ins width limit'.

22 Ignore left turn to South Street, continue **SA** towards Boughton. Follow road round sharp left-hand bend. At T-j turn **R** 'Boughton 1¼, Dunkirk 2'.

23 Pass beneath A2 then at T-j turn **L** 'Boughton ¼, Faversham 3¼'. After ¼ mile at next T-j at end of Colonel's Lane turn **L** through Boughton Street.

Ride 10 also passes through Shottenden & Chilham. Page 62

2 pages

Labyrinths of lanes, south of Canterbury

B y linking together back streets, alleys and footbridges, National Cycle Network Route 1 threads a safe route from the heart of the magnificent old centre of Canterbury out into the Kent countryside. Pass under the A2 and you soon join the labyrinth of wooded lanes that fill the triangle formed by Canterbury, Ashford and Dover. The ride runs almost due south through Petham, then follows a lovely quiet valley parallel with the old Roman Road of Stone Street, one of the few roads in this dense network that you are advised to avoid as it is fast and busy. Climb to the highpoint of the ride above Brabourne for the best views of the day out over Romney Marsh and the English Channel. After crossing Stone Street you are faced with a long climb, at times steep, through Postling and Etchinghill up to Shuttlesfield. The attractive village of Elham offers a variety of refreshment stops before plunging into the maze of lanes that have

a real feel of secret passages about them, weaving their way through the woodland north to Street End. One final climb and you are on the long gentle descent back down into Canterbury, rejoining the outward route near the A2 bridge. The delights

of Canterbury are best explored on foot: the city walls, medieval streets, St Augustine's Abbey, the ruins of the Norman castle and of course the cathedral, the mother church of the Anglican faith.

Overview

On-road ● 34 miles / 55 kilometres ● Moderate / Strenuous

Start
Royal Museum, High Street, Canterbury

Parking
If coming from outside Canterbury by car it is not worth driving into the centre of the city to start the ride. One option might be the Cow Lane car park on the A28, about 1 mile southeast of the centre, near Wincheap Industrial Estate. Take Hollow Lane opposite the car park then join the ride at **7**

Busy roads
● 'Minor' roads west of Etchinghill **16**

● 'Minor' road west of Street End **27**

Off-road sections
None, although some of the very narrow lanes have quite rough tarmac surfaces

Terrain
The land rises gently south from Canterbury. There are several climbs of 100-200ft (30-60m) and three longer ones

Nearest railway
Canterbury East

Refreshments
Canterbury
Lots of choice

Stowting
Tiger Inn
T: 01303 862130

Etchinghill
New Inn
T: 01303 862026

Elham
Lots of choice

Pett Bottom
Duck Inn
T: 01227 830354

Street End
Granville Inn
T: 01227 700402

Other rides nearby

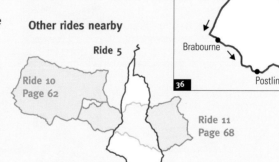

Ride 5

Ride 10
Page 62

Ride 11
Page 68

Map pages

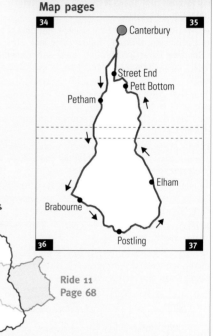

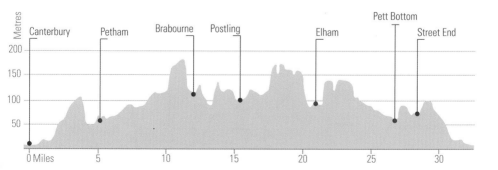

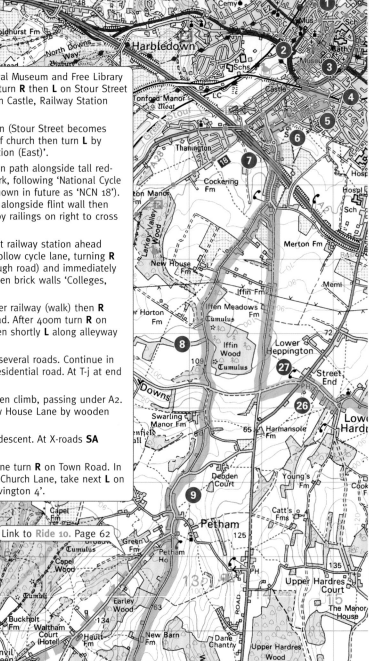

1 With your back to the Royal Museum and Free Library in Canterbury's High Street turn **R** then **L** on Stour Street 'St Mildred's Church, Norman Castle, Railway Station (East), Bike Route'.

2 Continue in same direction (Stour Street becomes Church Lane). Pass to left of church then turn **L** by metal bollards 'Railway Station (East)'.

3 At end of Gas Street **SA** on path alongside tall red-brick wall to right of car park, following 'National Cycle Network Route 18' signs (shown in future as 'NCN 18'). At next road go **SA** to pass alongside flint wall then **easy to miss** turn sharp **R** by railings on right to cross bridge over ring road.

4 At T-j with Canterbury East railway station ahead turn **L** 'Colleges, NCN 18'. Follow cycle lane, turning **R** on Rhodaus Close (no through road) and immediately **R** again on cyclepath between brick walls 'Colleges, Hospital'.

5 Turn **R** to cross bridge over railway (walk) then **R** again at T-j with Oxford Road. After 400m turn **R** on Lime Kiln Road 'NCN 18' then shortly **L** along alleyway between houses.

6 Follow alleyway crossing several roads. Continue in same direction as it joins residential road. At T-j at end of Hollowmede turn **L**.

7 At mini-roundabout **SA** then climb, passing under A2. After 1/2 mile first **R** on New House Lane by wooden bench 'Chartham 4'.

8 Long gentle climb, short descent. At X-roads **SA** 'Petham, Waltham'.

9 At T-j end of Watery Lane turn **R** on Town Road. In Petham, ignore first left on Church Lane, take next **L** on Duckpit Road 'Elmsted 4, Evington 4'.

2 pages →

Link to Ride 10. Page 62

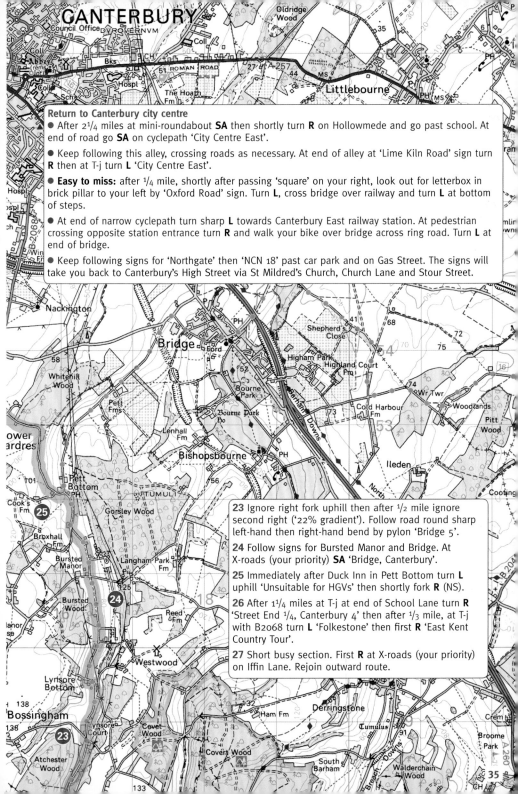

Return to Canterbury city centre

● After 2¼ miles at mini-roundabout **SA** then shortly turn **R** on Hollowmede and go past school. At end of road go **SA** on cyclepath 'City Centre East'.

● Keep following this alley, crossing roads as necessary. At end of alley at 'Lime Kiln Road' sign turn **R** then at T-j turn **L** 'City Centre East'.

● **Easy to miss:** after ¼ mile, shortly after passing 'square' on your right, look out for letterbox in brick pillar to your left by 'Oxford Road' sign. Turn **L**, cross bridge over railway and turn **L** at bottom of steps.

● At end of narrow cyclepath turn sharp **L** towards Canterbury East railway station. At pedestrian crossing opposite station entrance turn **R** and walk your bike over bridge across ring road. Turn **L** at end of bridge.

● Keep following signs for 'Northgate' then 'NCN 18' past car park and on Gas Street. The signs will take you back to Canterbury's High Street via St Mildred's Church, Church Lane and Stour Street.

23 Ignore right fork uphill then after ½ mile ignore second right ('22% gradient'). Follow road round sharp left-hand then right-hand bend by pylon 'Bridge 5'.

24 Follow signs for Bursted Manor and Bridge. At X-roads (your priority) **SA** 'Bridge, Canterbury'.

25 Immediately after Duck Inn in Pett Bottom turn **L** uphill 'Unsuitable for HGVs' then shortly fork **R** (NS).

26 After 1¼ miles at T-j at end of School Lane turn **R** 'Street End ¼, Canterbury 4' then after ⅓ mile, at T-j with B2068 turn **L** 'Folkestone' then first **R** 'East Kent Country Tour'.

27 Short busy section. First **R** at X-roads (your priority) on Iffin Lane. Rejoin outward route.

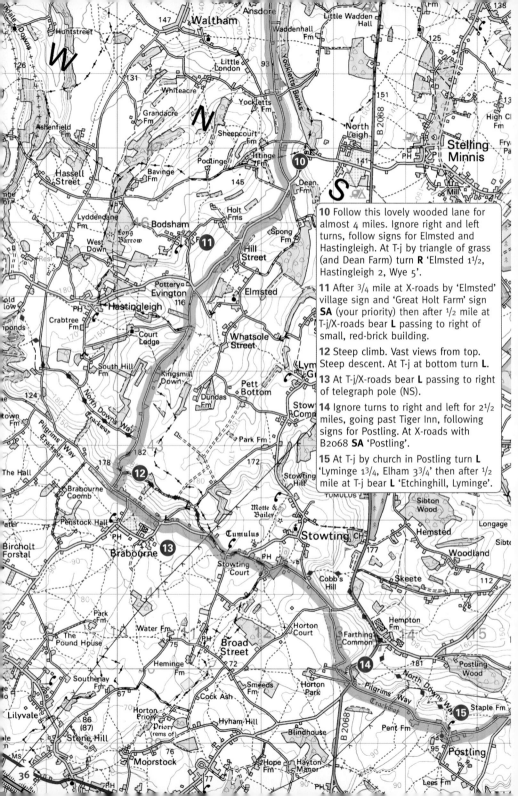

10 Follow this lovely wooded lane for almost 4 miles. Ignore right and left turns, follow signs for Elmsted and Hastingleigh. At T-j by triangle of grass (and Dean Farm) turn **R** 'Elmsted 1½, Hastingleigh 2, Wye 5'.

11 After ¾ mile at X-roads by 'Elmsted' village sign and 'Great Holt Farm' sign **SA** (your priority) then after ½ mile at T-j/X-roads bear **L** passing to right of small, red-brick building.

12 Steep climb. Vast views from top. Steep descent. At T-j at bottom turn **L**.

13 At T-j/X-roads bear **L** passing to right of telegraph pole (NS).

14 Ignore turns to right and left for 2½ miles, going past Tiger Inn, following signs for Postling. At X-roads with B2068 **SA** 'Postling'.

15 At T-j by church in Postling turn **L** 'Lyminge 1¾, Elham 3¾' then after ½ mile at T-j bear **L** 'Etchinghill, Lyminge'.

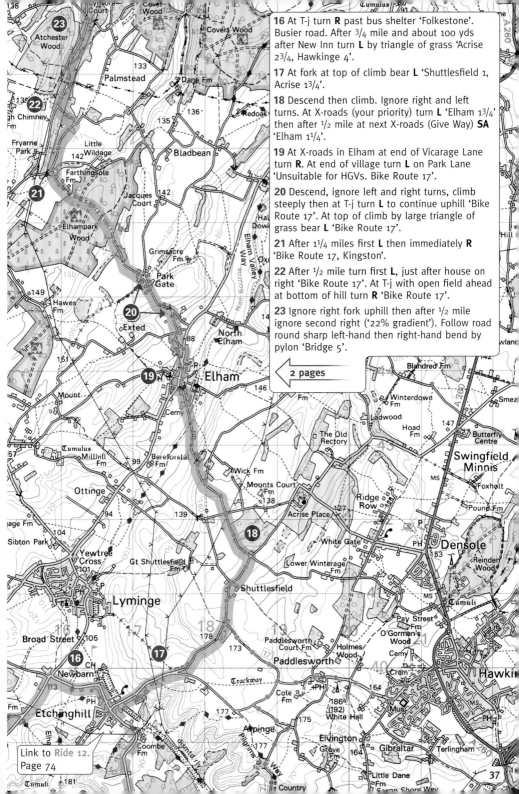

16 At T-j turn **R** past bus shelter 'Folkestone'. Busier road. After 3/4 mile and about 100 yds after New Inn turn **L** by triangle of grass 'Acrise 23/4, Hawkinge 4'.

17 At fork at top of climb bear **L** 'Shuttlesfield 1, Acrise 13/4'.

18 Descend then climb. Ignore right and left turns. At X-roads (your priority) turn **L** 'Elham 13/4' then after 1/2 mile at next X-roads (Give Way) **SA** 'Elham 11/4'.

19 At X-roads in Elham at end of Vicarage Lane turn **R**. At end of village turn **L** on Park Lane 'Unsuitable for HGVs. Bike Route 17'.

20 Descend, ignore left and right turns, climb steeply then at T-j turn **L** to continue uphill 'Bike Route 17'. At top of climb by large triangle of grass bear **L** 'Bike Route 17'.

21 After 11/4 miles first **L** then immediately **R** 'Bike Route 17, Kingston'.

22 After 1/2 mile turn first **L**, just after house on right 'Bike Route 17'. At T-j with open field ahead turn **R** 'Bike Route 17'.

23 Ignore right fork uphill then after 1/2 mile ignore second right ('22% gradient'). Follow road round sharp left-hand then right-hand bend by pylon 'Bridge 5'.

← 2 pages

Link to Ride 12.
Page 74

Through the orchards of Kent, west of Sandwich

The starting point for this ride is the attractive old town of Sandwich, one of the Cinque Ports (the others are Hastings, New Romney, Hythe and Dover), a confederation originally formed in the Middle Ages for military and trade purposes. Sandwich is a fascinating town with medieval streets and gateways. Queen Elizabeth I wined and dined at the Old House. As for the ride itself, there is a gentle tilt to the land from the start of the Kentish Downs in the southwest down to the coast to the north and east,

meaning the first half of the ride is steadily uphill and the second half largely downhill or flat. In its southeast corner the ride passes through the old coal-mining area of Kent, an industry that continued until the 1980s. Heading north the ride passes close to 18th century Goodnestone House, which boasts a walled rose garden and a fine array of rhododendrons and heathers. Jane Austen was a regular visitor and started work on *Pride & Prejudice* immediately after staying at Goodnestone in 1796. Continue north to drop down

into the Stour Valley, passing through the pretty village of Wickhambreaux. The best part of the ride is on the final section heading east on flat lanes through orchards of apples and pears on the edge of Ash Levels. Just before returning to Sandwich you pass the ruins of Rutupiae, or Richborough Castle, a Roman fortress built to guard Wantsum Channel from Saxon raiders. It was at Richborough that the Romans landed in AD 43.

Overview
On-road ● 29 miles / 47 kilometres ● Easy

Start
Centre of Sandwich

Parking
Several Pay & Display car parks in Sandwich

Busy roads
The 'minor' road between Wickhambreaux and Grove carries quite a lot of traffic
17 to **18**

Off-road sections
None

Terrain
Generally flat, with some gentle hills on the southern half of the ride

Nearest railway
Sandwich

Refreshments
Sandwich
Lots of choice

(East of) Eythorne
High & Dry PH
T: 01304 820545

Eythorne
Crown PH
T: 01304 830268

Chillenden
Griffins Head PH
T: 01304 840325

Ickham
Duke William PH
T: 01227 721308

Wickhambreaux
Rose Inn
T: 01227 721763

Preston
Half Moon PH
T: 01227 722296

Other rides nearby

Ride 6

Ride 7
Page 44

Map pages

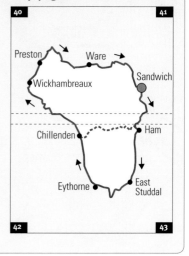

40   41

Preston   Ware

Wickhambreaux   Sandwich

Chillenden   Ham

Eythorne   East Studdal

42   43

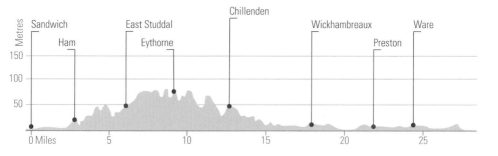

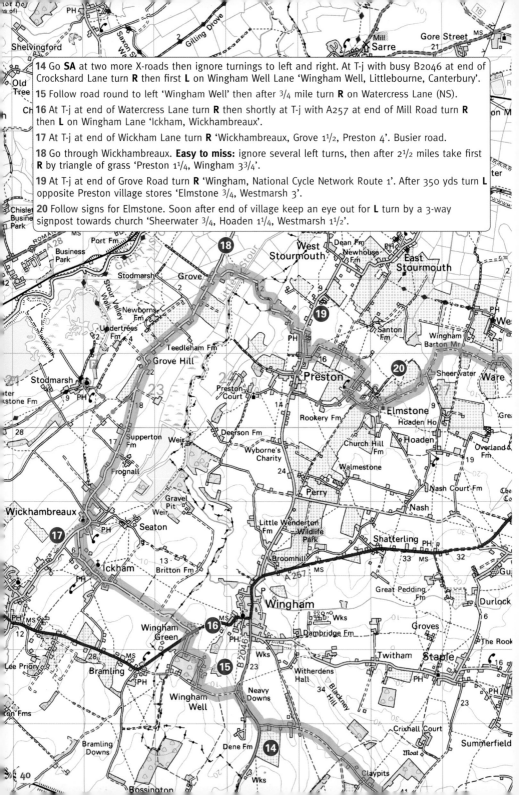

14 Go **SA** at two more X-roads then ignore turnings to left and right. At T-j with busy B2046 at end of Crockshard Lane turn **R** then first **L** on Wingham Well Lane 'Wingham Well, Littlebourne, Canterbury'.

15 Follow road round to left 'Wingham Well' then after 3/4 mile turn **R** on Watercress Lane (NS).

16 At T-j at end of Watercress Lane turn **R** then shortly at T-j with A257 at end of Mill Road turn **R** then **L** on Wingham Lane 'Ickham, Wickhambreaux'.

17 At T-j at end of Wickham Lane turn **R** 'Wickhambreaux, Grove 1 1/2, Preston 4'. Busier road.

18 Go through Wickhambreaux. **Easy to miss:** ignore several left turns, then after 2 1/2 miles take first **R** by triangle of grass 'Preston 1 1/4, Wingham 3 3/4'.

19 At T-j at end of Grove Road turn **R** 'Wingham, National Cycle Network Route 1'. After 350 yds turn **L** opposite Preston village stores 'Elmstone 3/4, Westmarsh 3'.

20 Follow signs for Elmstone. Soon after end of village keep an eye out for **L** turn by a 3-way signpost towards church 'Sheerwater 3/4, Hoaden 1 1/4, Westmarsh 1 1/2'.

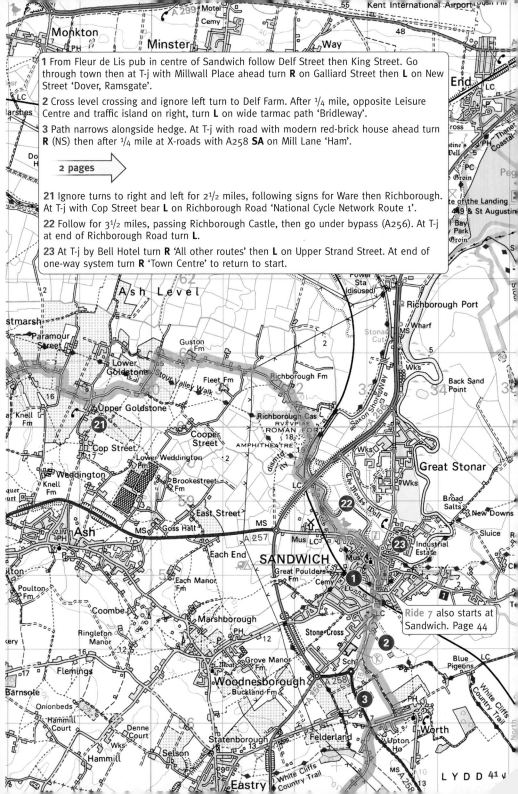

1 From Fleur de Lis pub in centre of Sandwich follow Delf Street then King Street. Go through town then at T-j with Millwall Place ahead turn **R** on Galliard Street then **L** on New Street 'Dover, Ramsgate'.

2 Cross level crossing and ignore left turn to Delf Farm. After ¼ mile, opposite Leisure Centre and traffic island on right, turn **L** on wide tarmac path 'Bridleway'.

3 Path narrows alongside hedge. At T-j with road with modern red-brick house ahead turn **R** (NS) then after ¼ mile at X-roads with A258 **SA** on Mill Lane 'Ham'.

2 pages ➡

21 Ignore turns to right and left for 2½ miles, following signs for Ware then Richborough. At T-j with Cop Street bear **L** on Richborough Road 'National Cycle Network Route 1'.

22 Follow for 3½ miles, passing Richborough Castle, then go under bypass (A256). At T-j at end of Richborough Road turn **L**.

23 At T-j by Bell Hotel turn **R** 'All other routes' then **L** on Upper Strand Street. At end of one-way system turn **R** 'Town Centre' to return to start.

Ride 7 also starts at Sandwich. Page 44

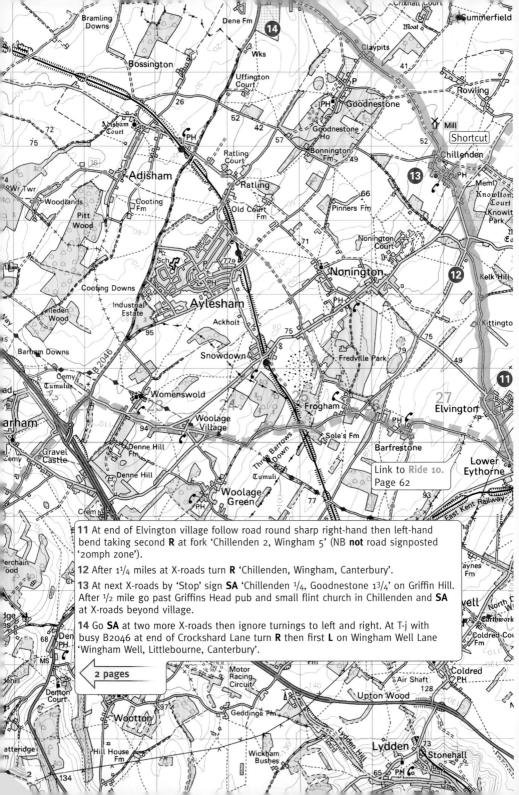

11 At end of Elvington village follow road round sharp right-hand then left-hand bend taking second **R** at fork 'Chillenden 2, Wingham 5' (NB **not** road signposted '20mph zone').

12 After 1¼ miles at X-roads turn **R** 'Chillenden, Wingham, Canterbury'.

13 At next X-roads by 'Stop' sign **SA** 'Chillenden ¼, Goodnestone 1¾' on Griffin Hill. After ½ mile go past Griffins Head pub and small flint church in Chillenden and **SA** at X-roads beyond village.

14 Go **SA** at two more X-roads then ignore turnings to left and right. At T-j with busy B2046 at end of Crockshard Lane turn **R** then first **L** on Wingham Well Lane 'Wingham Well, Littlebourne, Canterbury'.

Link to Ride 10. Page 62

← 2 pages

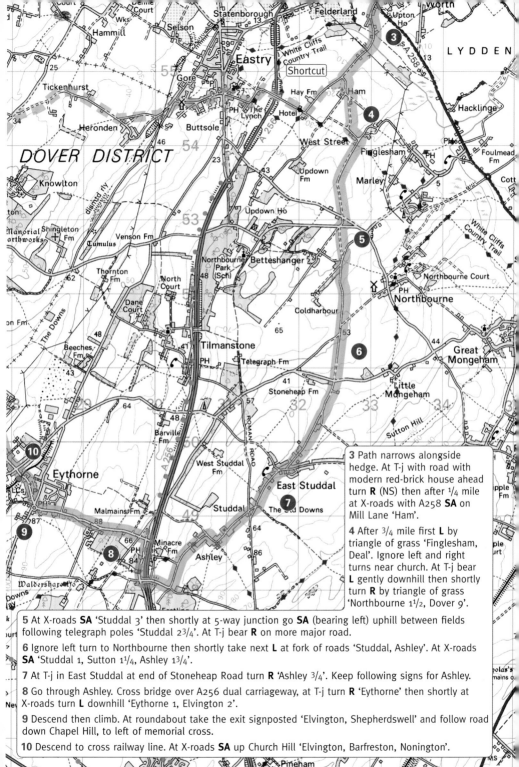

3 Path narrows alongside hedge. At T-j with road with modern red-brick house ahead turn **R** (NS) then after 1/4 mile at X-roads with A258 **SA** on Mill Lane 'Ham'.

4 After 3/4 mile first **L** by triangle of grass 'Finglesham, Deal'. Ignore left and right turns near church. At T-j bear **L** gently downhill then shortly turn **R** by triangle of grass 'Northbourne 1 1/2, Dover 9'.

5 At X-roads **SA** 'Studdal 3' then shortly at 5-way junction go **SA** (bearing left) uphill between fields following telegraph poles 'Studdal 2 3/4'. At T-j bear **R** on more major road.

6 Ignore left turn to Northbourne then shortly take next **L** at fork of roads 'Studdal, Ashley'. At X-roads **SA** 'Studdal 1, Sutton 1 1/4, Ashley 1 3/4'.

7 At T-j in East Studdal at end of Stoneheap Road turn **R** 'Ashley 3/4'. Keep following signs for Ashley.

8 Go through Ashley. Cross bridge over A256 dual carriageway, at T-j turn **R** 'Eythorne' then shortly at X-roads turn **L** downhill 'Eythorne 1, Elvington 2'.

9 Descend then climb. At roundabout take the exit signposted 'Elvington, Shepherdswell' and follow road down Chapel Hill, to left of memorial cross.

10 Descend to cross railway line. At X-roads **SA** up Church Hill 'Elvington, Barfreston, Nonington'.

Sandwich, Deal & the Straits of Dover

With its myriad of old buildings, Sandwich is a beautiful, medieval town well worth exploring on foot, before or after the ride. Exit the town on a toll road (free for bikes) that takes you past sand dunes and the Royal Cinque Ports Golf Club. This leads on to Deal with big views out over the Straits of Dover from the seafront. Fishing boats and lobster pots form a picturesque foreground on the shingle beach. On the southern edge of Deal lies Walmer Castle, built as a Tudor rose-shaped fort by Henry VIII and converted in the 18th century as the official residence of the Lords Warden of the Cinque Ports. The ride follows a traffic-free trail from the south end of Deal alongside the coast to Kingsdown. Here you turn inland and are faced with the only long climb of the ride, with the steepest bit at the start. After skirting the north edge of Whitfield, turn northwest, aiming for the amazing 12th century church

in Barfrestone with particularly striking stone carving around the main door on its south side, said to be the finest Norman stonework in England. The church has no tower but the bell hangs in a nearby yew tree! After crossing the old coal-mining areas of Kent you enter an area which

seems to be bursting with fertility – there are orchards of all types, vineyards, maize, cereal crops and long lines of polytunnels for the cultivation of soft fruit. A bridge over the A256 brings you safely back into Sandwich.

Overview
On-road ● 31 miles / 50 kilometres ● Easy

Start
The Bell Hotel in the centre
of Sandwich

Parking
Several Pay & Display car
parks in Sandwich

Busy roads
The ride uses streets through
Sandwich ❶ and ㉖ and
Deal ❺

Off-road sections
Short gravel section between
Deal and Kingsdown ❻

Terrain
The northern half of the ride is
flatter than the southern half

Nearest railway
Sandwich

Refreshments
Sandwich
Lots of choice

Deal
Lots of choice

West Cliffe
Red Lion PH
T: 01304 852467

Guston
Chance Inn
T: 01304 206162

Barfrestone
Yew Tree Inn
T: 01304 831000

Woodnesborough
Poacher PH
T: 01304 613189

Other rides nearby

Map pages

Ride 6
Page 38

Ride 7

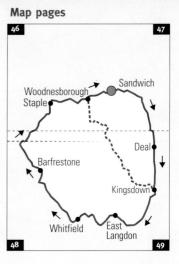

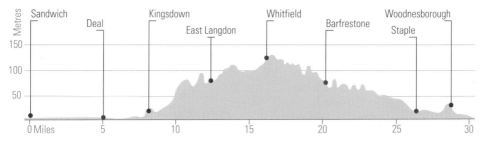

23 After 1 mile at T-j turn **R** 'Staple, Ash'.

24 Keep following signs for Staple and Ash at several junctions. At offset X-roads in Staple at end of Buckland Lane turn **L** then **R** on School Lane.

25 At X-roads turn **L** 'Woodnesborough 1, Ash 2, Sandwich 2'.

DOVER DISTRICT

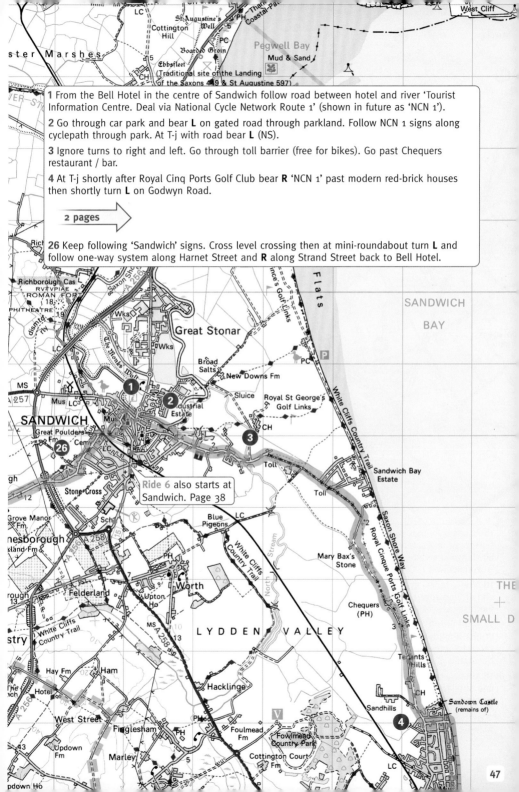

1 From the Bell Hotel in the centre of Sandwich follow road between hotel and river 'Tourist Information Centre. Deal via National Cycle Network Route 1' (shown in future as 'NCN 1').

2 Go through car park and bear **L** on gated road through parkland. Follow NCN 1 signs along cyclepath through park. At T-j with road bear **L** (NS).

3 Ignore turns to right and left. Go through toll barrier (free for bikes). Go past Chequers restaurant / bar.

4 At T-j shortly after Royal Cinq Ports Golf Club bear **R** 'NCN 1' past modern red-brick houses then shortly turn **L** on Godwyn Road.

2 pages ⟹

26 Keep following 'Sandwich' signs. Cross level crossing then at mini-roundabout turn **L** and follow one-way system along Harnet Street and **R** along Strand Street back to Bell Hotel.

Ride 6 also starts at Sandwich. Page 38

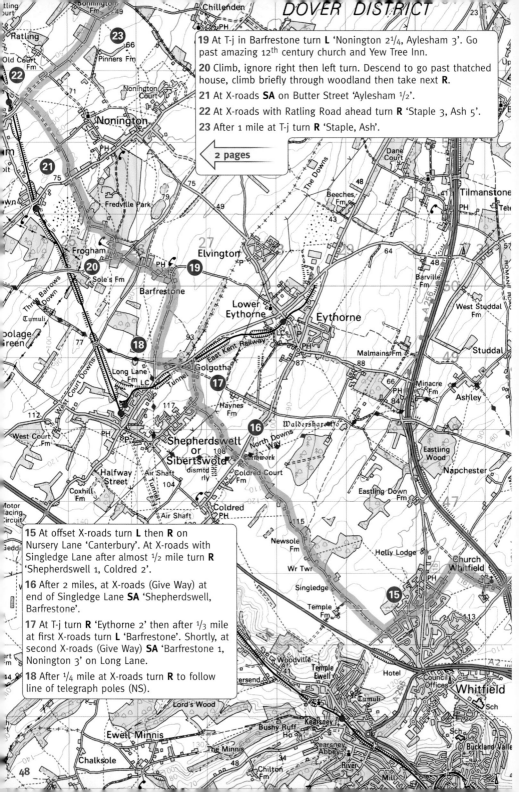

19 At T-j in Barfrestone turn **L** 'Nonington 2¼, Aylesham 3'. Go past amazing 12th century church and Yew Tree Inn.

20 Climb, ignore right then left turn. Descend to go past thatched house, climb briefly through woodland then take next **R**.

21 At X-roads **SA** on Butter Street 'Aylesham ½'.

22 At X-roads with Ratling Road ahead turn **R** 'Staple 3, Ash 5'.

23 After 1 mile at T-j turn **R** 'Staple, Ash'.

← **2 pages**

15 At offset X-roads turn **L** then **R** on Nursery Lane 'Canterbury'. At X-roads with Singledge Lane after almost ½ mile turn **R** 'Shepherdswell 1, Coldred 2'.

16 After 2 miles, at X-roads (Give Way) at end of Singledge Lane **SA** 'Shepherdswell, Barfrestone'.

17 At T-j turn **R** 'Eythorne 2' then after ⅓ mile at first X-roads turn **L** 'Barfrestone'. Shortly, at second X-roads (Give Way) **SA** 'Barfrestone 1, Nonington 3' on Long Lane.

18 After ¼ mile at X-roads turn **R** to follow line of telegraph poles (NS).

48

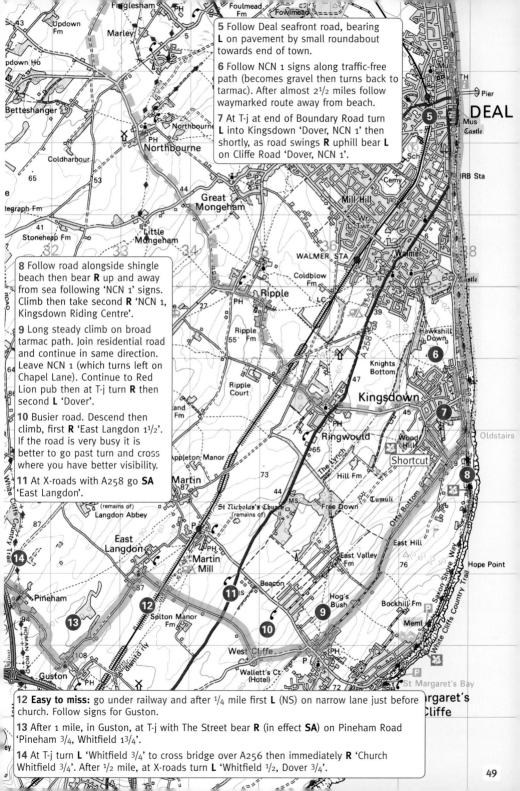

5 Follow Deal seafront road, bearing **L** on pavement by small roundabout towards end of town.

6 Follow NCN 1 signs along traffic-free path (becomes gravel then turns back to tarmac). After almost 2¹/₂ miles follow waymarked route away from beach.

7 At T-j at end of Boundary Road turn **L** into Kingsdown 'Dover, NCN 1' then shortly, as road swings **R** uphill bear **L** on Cliffe Road 'Dover, NCN 1'.

8 Follow road alongside shingle beach then bear **R** up and away from sea following 'NCN 1' signs. Climb then take second **R** 'NCN 1, Kingsdown Riding Centre'.

9 Long steady climb on broad tarmac path. Join residential road and continue in same direction. Leave NCN 1 (which turns left on Chapel Lane). Continue to Red Lion pub then at T-j turn **R** then second **L** 'Dover'.

10 Busier road. Descend then climb, first **R** 'East Langdon 1¹/₂'. If the road is very busy it is better to go past turn and cross where you have better visibility.

11 At X-roads with A258 go **SA** 'East Langdon'.

12 Easy to miss: go under railway and after ¹/₄ mile first **L** (NS) on narrow lane just before church. Follow signs for Guston.

13 After 1 mile, in Guston, at T-j with The Street bear **R** (in effect **SA**) on Pineham Road 'Pineham ³/₄, Whitfield 1³/₄'.

14 At T-j turn **L** 'Whitfield ³/₄' to cross bridge over A256 then immediately **R** 'Church Whitfield ³/₄'. After ¹/₂ mile, at X-roads turn **L** 'Whitfield ¹/₂, Dover ³/₄'.

Headcorn & the North Downs

The fine town of Headcorn is set at the heart of a network of lanes offering numerous options for shorter or longer rides. The lanes lying to the east of the A274 tend to be quieter and these are explored in this ride. Tiny lanes barely wider than a vehicle lead north, climbing then descending past the estate of Leeds Castle. The castle was built in the 12th century by Robert de Crevecoeur and became a royal palace for King Edward I. It was transformed by Henry VIII for his first wife, Catherine of Aragon. It has been open to the public since 1976. Back on the ride, a pavement conveniently offers an alternative to the short time spent on the A20. Pass under the M20 and over two railway lines on your way to Hollingbourne. The Dirty Habit pub, with its signboard featuring a monk, is located on the North Downs Way, also known as Pilgrims Way as it was used by pilgrims on their way to Canterbury. Chaucer and all that! A short, steep climb from Broad Street to Hucking takes you up the face of the North Downs escarpment with ever better views opening up behind you. Coppiced woodland gives way to fruit orchards as you navigate your way through the maze of lanes that spread like tendrils across the countryside. There are few areas of Britain that have such a dense network of lanes as exist between Chatham and Dover. Small villages with pubs at Bredgar, Doddington, Warren Street and Charing Heath are like beacons guiding you through the labyrinth back to Headcorn.

Overview
On-road ● 36 miles / 58 kilometres ● Moderate

Start
George & Dragon pub,
Headcorn, southeast
of Maidstone

Parking
Pay & Display car park in
Headcorn – follow signs

Busy roads
About ¼ mile on A20 near
Leeds Castle (there is a
pavement) **6**

Off-road sections
None

Terrain
Undulating with several climbs
of 100-200ft (30-60m) and
three longer ones

Nearest railway
Headcorn

Refreshments
Headcorn
Lots of choice

Hollingbourne
Dirty Habit PH
T: 01622 880880

Hucking
Hook & Hatchet PH
T: 01622 880830

Doddington
Chequers Inn
T: 01795 886366

Warren Street
Harrow PH
T: 01622 858727

(near) Charing Hill
Bowl Inn
T: 01233 712256

Charing Heath
Red Lion PH
T: 01233 712418

Other rides nearby

Ride 4
Page 26

Ride 8

Ride 10
Page 62

Ride 9
Page 56

Map pages

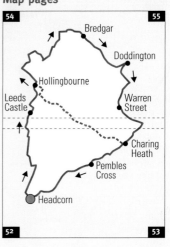

54   55

Bredgar
Doddington
Hollingbourne
Leeds
Castle
Warren
Street
Charing
Heath
Pembles
Cross
Headcorn

52   53

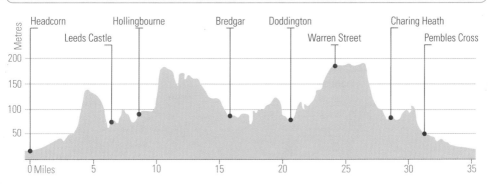

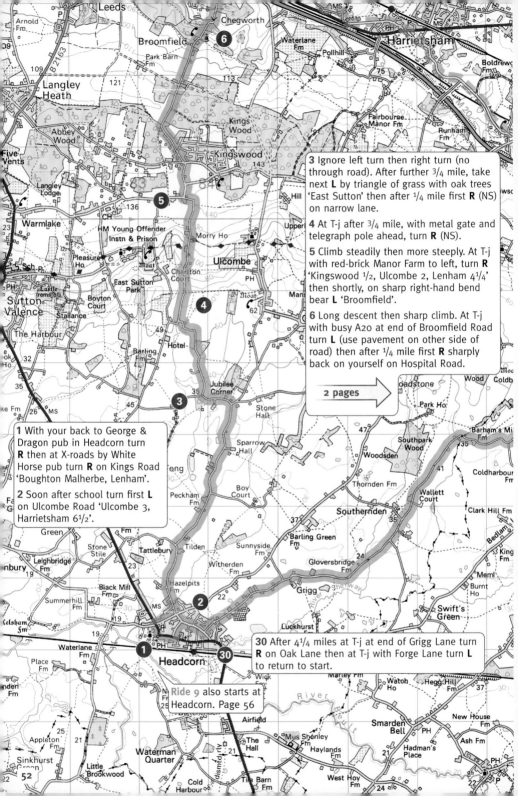

3 Ignore left turn then right turn (no through road). After further 3/4 mile, take next **L** by triangle of grass with oak trees 'East Sutton' then after 1/4 mile first **R** (NS) on narrow lane.

4 At T-j after 3/4 mile, with metal gate and telegraph pole ahead, turn **R** (NS).

5 Climb steadily then more steeply. At T-j with red-brick Manor Farm to left, turn **R** 'Kingswood 1/2, Ulcombe 2, Lenham 4 1/4' then shortly, on sharp right-hand bend bear **L** 'Broomfield'.

6 Long descent then sharp climb. At T-j with busy A20 at end of Broomfield Road turn **L** (use pavement on other side of road) then after 1/4 mile first **R** sharply back on yourself on Hospital Road.

2 pages

1 With your back to George & Dragon pub in Headcorn turn **R** then at X-roads by White Horse pub turn **R** on Kings Road 'Boughton Malherbe, Lenham'.

2 Soon after school turn first **L** on Ulcombe Road 'Ulcombe 3, Harrietsham 6 1/2'.

30 After 4 1/4 miles at T-j at end of Grigg Lane turn **R** on Oak Lane then at T-j with Forge Lane turn **L** to return to start.

Ride 9 also starts at Headcorn. Page 56

52

Link to Ride 10.
Page 62

24 After almost 2 miles at X-roads (Give Way) by Bowl pub turn **R**.

25 Steep descent. At X-roads with A20 **SA** 'Charing Heath, Egerton'.

26 At T-j by Red Lion pub in Charing Heath bear **R** 'Egerton 2'.

27 Cross bridge over M20. Ignore left turn to Southfield then shortly take next **R** (NS) opposite stone wall on left.

28 After ½ mile, at fork bear **R** on upper lane. Shortly, ignore Coach Road to right.

29 At T-j at end of Egerton House Road turn **L** 'Egerton 2, Charing 7' then bear **R** (Barham's Mill Road).

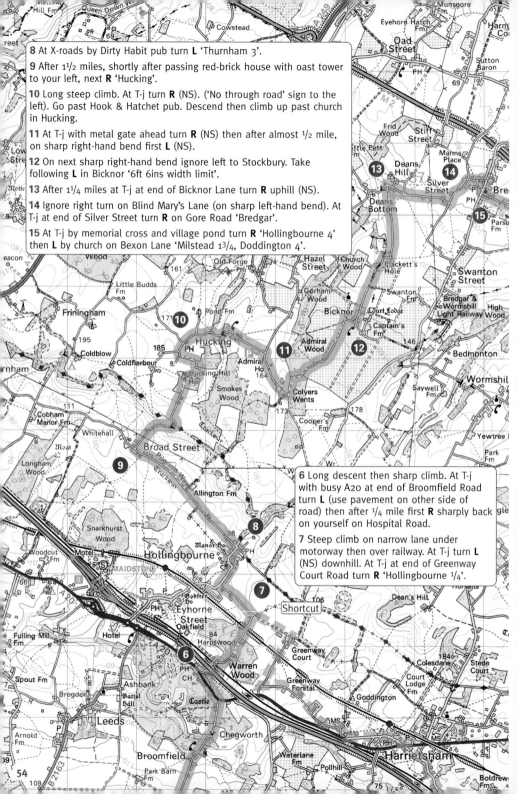

8 At X-roads by Dirty Habit pub turn **L** 'Thurnham 3'.

9 After 1½ miles, shortly after passing red-brick house with oast tower to your left, next **R** 'Hucking'.

10 Long steep climb. At T-j turn **R** (NS). ('No through road' sign to the left). Go past Hook & Hatchet pub. Descend then climb up past church in Hucking.

11 At T-j with metal gate ahead turn **R** (NS) then after almost ½ mile, on sharp right-hand bend first **L** (NS).

12 On next sharp right-hand bend ignore left to Stockbury. Take following **L** in Bicknor '6ft 6ins width limit'.

13 After 1¼ miles at T-j at end of Bicknor Lane turn **R** uphill (NS).

14 Ignore right turn on Blind Mary's Lane (on sharp left-hand bend). At T-j at end of Silver Street turn **R** on Gore Road 'Bredgar'.

15 At T-j by memorial cross and village pond turn **R** 'Hollingbourne 4' then **L** by church on Bexon Lane 'Milstead 1¾, Doddington 4'.

6 Long descent then sharp climb. At T-j with busy A20 at end of Broomfield Road turn **L** (use pavement on other side of road) then after ¼ mile first **R** sharply back on yourself on Hospital Road.

7 Steep climb on narrow lane under motorway then over railway. At T-j turn **L** (NS) downhill. At T-j at end of Greenway Court Road turn **R** 'Hollingbourne ¼'.

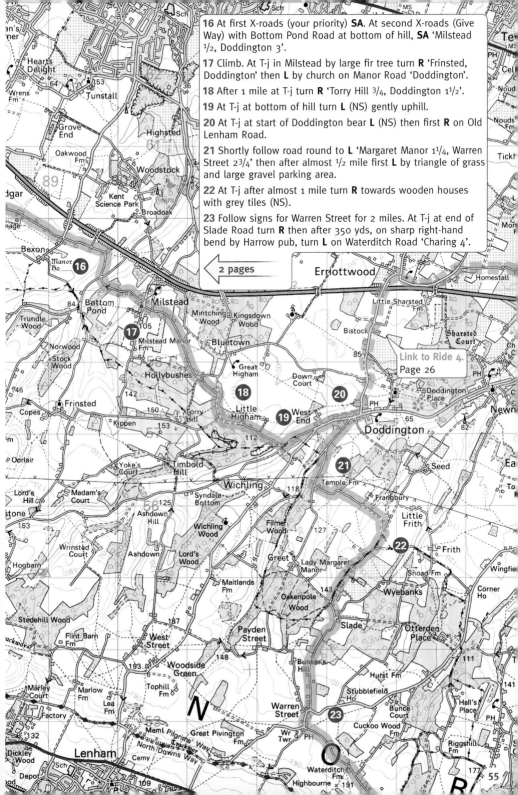

16 At first X-roads (your priority) **SA**. At second X-roads (Give Way) with Bottom Pond Road at bottom of hill, **SA** 'Milstead ½, Doddington 3'.

17 Climb. At T-j in Milstead by large fir tree turn **R** 'Frinsted, Doddington' then **L** by church on Manor Road 'Doddington'.

18 After 1 mile at T-j turn **R** 'Torry Hill ¾, Doddington 1½'.

19 At T-j at bottom of hill turn **L** (NS) gently uphill.

20 At T-j at start of Doddington bear **L** (NS) then first **R** on Old Lenham Road.

21 Shortly follow road round to **L** 'Margaret Manor 1¼, Warren Street 2¾' then after almost ½ mile first **L** by triangle of grass and large gravel parking area.

22 At T-j after almost 1 mile turn **R** towards wooden houses with grey tiles (NS).

23 Follow signs for Warren Street for 2 miles. At T-j at end of Slade Road turn **R** then after 350 yds, on sharp right-hand bend by Harrow pub, turn **L** on Waterditch Road 'Charing 4'.

← 2 pages

Link to Ride 4.
Page 26

Headcorn, Pluckley & Sissinghurst

As mentioned in the previous ride, Headcorn is an excellent base for road rides – it has plenty of pubs and cafés (as well as a bike shop) and the village is surrounded by a dense network of relatively flat lanes between the North Downs to the north and the High Weald to the west. This ride links Headcorn to the attractive village of Smarden, an ancient centre of the wool trade with many fine half-timbered weatherboarded houses. Climbing from here to a mighty 330ft (100m), Pluckley is the highest point on the whole trip, giving you an idea of how easy the gradients are. Pluckley is said to be the most haunted village in England. The TV comedy saga *The Darling Buds of May* was filmed here. The ride weaves its way south to the handsome windmill at Woodchurch before turning west on tiny quiet lanes through St Michaels towards Sissinghurst. Here you have a choice: the most memorable option takes you right past Sissinghurst Castle, a Tudor

mansion with one of the loveliest gardens in England, created by Vita Sackville-West and Harold Nicholson in the 1930s. This route does, however, commit you to about 1/2 mile on a stone and grass bridleway to link up with the lane network to the

north. If you wish to avoid this there is a road alternative via Sissinghurst village and the road to Frittenden. The two routes link again near Bettenham Manor and use the quietest approach back into Headcorn via Lashenden and Waterman Quarter.

Overview
On-road ● 35 miles / 56 kilometres ● Easy

Start
George & Dragon pub,
Headcorn, southeast
of Maidstone

Parking
Pay & Display car park in
Headcorn – follow signs

Busy roads
● About ¹/₂ mile on A28 east
of Bethersden **6**

● About ¹/₂ mile on A262 east
of Sissinghurst village (there is
a pavement) **13**

Off-road sections
About ¹/₂ mile of stone / grass
bridleway north of Sissinghurst
Castle (there is a longer, quiet
lane alternative via Sissinghurst
village) **14** to **15**

Terrain
Gently undulating, with only
one noticeable hill

Nearest railway
Headcorn

Refreshments
Headcorn
Lots of choice

Smarden Bell
Bell Inn
T: 01233 770283

Smarden
Chequers Inn
T: 01233 770217

Pluckley
Black Horse PH
T: 01233 840256

Woodchurch
Bonny Cravat PH
T: 01233 860345

Sissinghurst
Bull Inn
T: 01580 712821

Sissinghurst Castle Café
Shut Wednesdays
& Thursdays
T: 01580 710701

Other rides nearby

Ride 8
Page 50

Ride 9

Ride 13
Page 80

Map pages

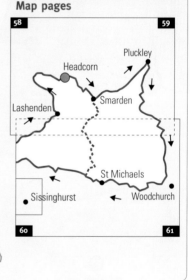

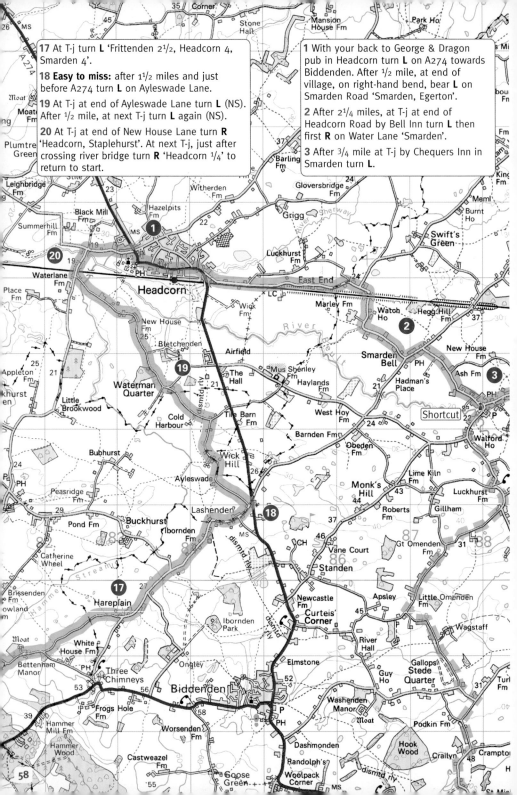

17 At T-j turn **L** 'Frittenden 2½, Headcorn 4, Smarden 4'.

18 Easy to miss: after 1½ miles and just before A274 turn **L** on Ayleswade Lane.

19 At T-j at end of Ayleswade Lane turn **L** (NS). After ½ mile, at next T-j turn **L** again (NS).

20 At T-j at end of New House Lane turn **R** 'Headcorn, Staplehurst'. At next T-j, just after crossing river bridge turn **R** 'Headcorn ¼' to return to start.

1 With your back to George & Dragon pub in Headcorn turn **L** on A274 towards Biddenden. After ½ mile, at end of village, on right-hand bend, bear **L** on Smarden Road 'Smarden, Egerton'.

2 After 2¼ miles, at T-j at end of Headcorn Road by Bell Inn turn **L** then first **R** on Water Lane 'Smarden'.

3 After ¾ mile at T-j by Chequers Inn in Smarden turn **L**.

4 After almost 4 miles at top of hill in Pluckley turn **R** 'Village shops, Bethersden 4'.

5 Follow signs for Bethersden, crossing railway bridge. **Easy to miss:** after 3½ miles, at X-roads (your priority) just after 'Bethersden' village sign **SA** 'Great Chart 4, Ashford 5' then take next **R** on Kiln Lane.

6 At T-j with very busy A28 at end of Kiln Lane turn **L** then first **R** 'Woodchurch 3' (**TAKE CARE**).

Link to Ride 10.
Page 62

2 pages

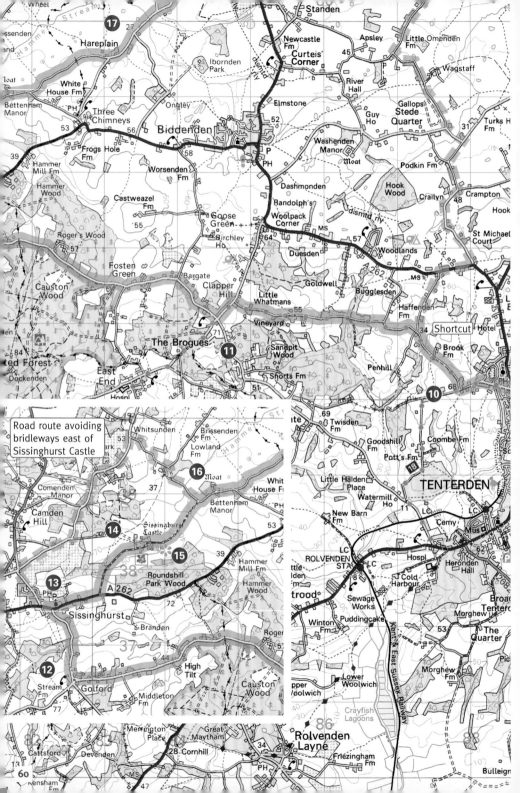

Road route avoiding bridleways east of Sissinghurst Castle

6 At T-j with very busy A28 at end of Kiln Lane turn **L** then first **R** 'Woodchurch 3' (**TAKE CARE**).

7 Easy to miss: follow signs for Woodchurch for 3 miles through two X-roads. Shortly after passing windmill and '30mph' signs at start of Woodchurch take next **R** on Susans Hill 'Woodchurch Museum, St Michaels 5'.

8 Again, **easy to miss:** follow road round two sharp bends, ignoring turns on each bend. Take next **R** (NS) by long, low barn with a round roof. Shortly, at T-j by triangle of grass and wooden shed turn **R** (NS).

9 After 2½ miles at T-j with busy A28 in St Michaels turn **R** then **L** by Crown pub.

10 After ½ mile turn **R** on Readers Bridge Road 'National Cycle Network Route 18, Tunbridge Wells' by Honour Silcocks Farm Shop.

11 Ignore two right turns. Shortly after Biddenden Vineyard, at T-j at end of Gribble Bridge Road, turn **L** 'National Cycle Network Route 18' then at X-roads **R** 'Cranbrook, Goudhurst'.

12 After 3½ miles at X-roads with red-brick bungalow in triangle of grass turn **R** 'Sissinghurst'.

13 At T-j with A262 by Bull Inn in Sissinghurst turn **R***. Use pavement with discretion. After almost ½ mile first **L** 'Sissinghurst Garden National Trust'.

* For road alternative avoiding short bridleway section, at Bull Inn turn **L** then first **R** on Common Road 'Frittenden'.

14 Go past Sissinghurst Castle car park towards coffee shop and plant shop. Pass to right of oast houses then between shop and castle on wide gravel track.

15 As gravel track swings right following moat, bear **L** (in effect **SA**) on earth and stone track. Descend then climb. Rough track lasts for ½ mile - you may prefer to walk.

16 At T-j with road by metal barrier turn **R** then shortly first **L** (NS) by small triangle of grass.

17 At T-j turn **L** 'Frittenden 2½, Headcorn 4, Smarden 4'.

Ride 13 also passes through Woodchurch. Page 80

2 pages

West of Wye on the North Downs

As with Headcorn, the starting point for the previous ride, Wye is just the right sized place to be based for a weekend, with a railway station right on the doorstep and several options for accommodation, pubs and cafés. It has lanes radiating out to the four points of the compass and is surrounded by attractive downland put to a mixture of use, from woodland to cereal crops, grazing pasture and fruit orchards. Of all the exits from Wye, those to the west

are likely to be busiest so be prepared for some traffic on the first couple of miles. Once beyond the A251 the ride enters a different world of tiny quiet lanes through beautiful Kentish countryside. As you approach Charing you should catch a glimpse of the windmill up on the horizon. This is reached via a very steep climb up the chalk escarpment of the North Downs, taking you past the highest point on the whole ride. There is a lovely descent down what feels like

a secret valley after Stalisfield church. The next highlight is Chilham with its castle and lovely square surrounded by fine half-timbered buildings. Descend to cross the Great Stour River and use a track around a lake, thus conveniently avoiding the busy A28. There is no quiet route down the valley so you are faced with one last climb back up past orchards and coppiced woodland, taking in the remote Compasses Inn at Sole Street before returning back to Wye.

Overview

On-road ● 30 miles / 48 kilometres ● Moderate

Start
Wye, about 4 miles north of Ashford

Parking
Follow signs, or there is plenty of street parking

Busy roads
● 1 mile on the 'minor' road from Wye to the A28 **3**

● Use the pavement for 1 mile alongside the A251 south of Boughton Lees **5** to **6**

● About 200yds on the A252 west of Chilham **21**

Off-road sections
1/2 mile on wide gravel track around the lake east of Chilham **22** to **23**

Terrain
Undulating, cut through by the Great Stour River. Several climbs of 100-200ft (30-60m) and two longer ones

Nearest railway
Wye

Refreshments
Wye
Lots of choice

Boughton Lees
Flying Horse PH
T: 01233 620914

Westwell
Wheel Inn
T: 01233 712430

Chilham
Lots of choice

Sole Street
Compasses Inn
T: 01227 700300

Map pages

Other rides nearby

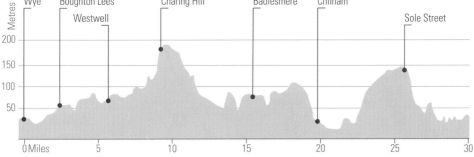

Ride 4 also passes through Shottenden. Page 26

Ride 11 also starts at Wye. Page 68

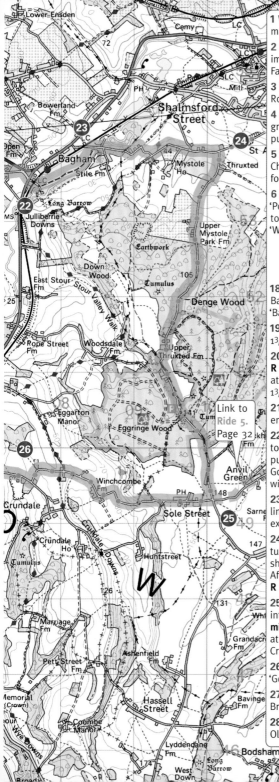

1 With your back to church in Wye go **SA** down main street (Church Street). At T-j turn **R** (NS).

2 Cross bridge then level crossing, and turn immediately **L** on Harville Road 'Ashford 4, Faversham 12'.

3 Busy road. At X-roads with A28 at end of Harville Road **SA** 'Boughton Lees'.

4 After 3/4 mile take first **L** at start of large village green in Boughton Lees, just before Flying Horse pub.

5 Shortly, at T-j with A251 by St Christopher's Church turn **L**. Cross to other side of road and follow pavement alongside wall.

6 After almost 1 mile turn **R** on Sandyhurst Lane 'Potters Corner, Westwell', passing an ornate gate tower on right. Shortly first **R** on Lenacre Street 'Westwell'.

2 pages

18 At T-j with busy Ashford Road (A251) at end of Bagshill Road turn **L** then first **R** on Dayton Street 'Badlesmere Court, Fisher Street, Molash'.

19 At T-j bear **R** uphill 'Fisher Street 1/2, Shottenden 13/4, Chilham 31/4'.

20 Ignore several turns to right and left. At T-j turn **R** 'Shottenden 1/2, Chilham 2' then after 1/3 mile at X-roads at end of Goldups Lane turn **L** 'Chilham 13/4, Canterbury 8'.

21 At T-j with A252 at bottom of long descent at end of Soles Hill Road turn **L** then first **R**.

22 Climb to Chilham's Square and go diagonally **L** to far corner (The Street). Descend past Woolpack pub. At X-roads with A28 **SA** 'Mid Kent Fisheries'. Go over level crossing and immediately turn **L** on wide gravel track.

23 Follow track between lake on right and railway line on left. After 1/2 mile as track turns sharp right, exit via metal gate on lane and turn **R**.

24 Cross small bridge over river and ignore right turn (no through road). Climb, following road round sharp left-hand bend by 'Byway / Bridleway' sign. After 1/4 mile ignore left turn then shortly take next **R** on Penny Pot Lane 'Sole Street, Waltham'.

25 Long steady climb past orchard on right then into sweet chestnut coppice woodland. **Easy to miss:** 31/2 miles after turning onto Penny Pot Lane, at X-roads (your priority) turn **R** 'Sole Street 1/4, Crundale 11/2'.

26 Long descent, short climb. At T-j turn **R** 'Godmersham 13/4, Wye 23/4'.

27 After almost 3/4 mile at next T-j turn **L** 'Wye 21/4, Brook 5'.

28 After 2 miles at X-roads in Wye at end of Olantigh Road turn **R** to return to start.

Link to Ride 5. Page 32

5 Shortly, at T-j with A251 by St Christopher's Church turn **L**. Cross to other side of road and follow pavement alongside wall.

6 After almost 1 mile turn **R** on Sandyhurst Lane 'Potters Corner, Westwell', passing an ornate gate tower on right. Shortly first **R** on Lenacre Street 'Westwell'.

7 Ignore left to Potters Corner. After almost 1 mile as road swings sharp left by the Wheel Inn in Westwell, continue **SA** 'Charing 3³/₄, Maidstone 16¹/₄'.

8 Ignore first right after ¹/₂ mile. Almost 1 mile after Wheel Inn, on sharp left-hand bend take next **R** by triangle of grass 'Charing 2¹/₂'.

9 After ³/₄ mile at fork by triangle of grass bear **R** (NS).

10 After ¹/₂ mile at T-j turn **R** and follow road round left-hand bend. Immediately after passing huge red-brick mansion of Pett Place turn **R** uphill alongside red-brick wall.

11 Shortly, at T-j by triangle of grass with tree growing in it turn **L** (NS) then after ¹/₂ mile at T-j with busy A252 at end of Pilgrims Way, cross road onto opposite pavement and turn **R** uphill. Take first **L** on The Wyns.

12 Very steep climb. At T-j at top turn **L** (NS) then after almost ¹/₂ mile first **R** 'Stalisfield Church 1³/₄'.

13 At T-j turn **R** 'Stalisfield Church' then first **L** (same sign).

14 Go past Stalisfield Church, ignore left to Stalisfield Green then shortly at fork bear **L** 'Faversham 7'.

15 At X-roads (your priority) on long descent **SA** 'Faversham 5'.

16 Continue to bottom of descent by red-brick Southern Water building, start to climb then after 350 yds first **R** on Haywards Hill 'Belmont ³/₄, Throwley 1, Sheldwich 2'.

17 Ignore first left at top of climb. On sharp right-hand bend next **L** on Bagshill Road 'Badlesmere 3, Sheldwich 4'.

18 At T-j with busy Ashford Road (A251) at end of Bagshill Road turn **L** then first **R** on Dayton Street 'Badlesmere Court, Fisher Street, Molash'.

19 At T-j bear **R** uphill 'Fisher Street ¹/₂, Shottenden 1³/₄, Chilham 3¹/₄'.

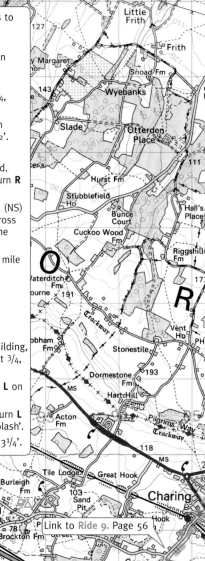

2 pages

Link to Ride 9. Page 56

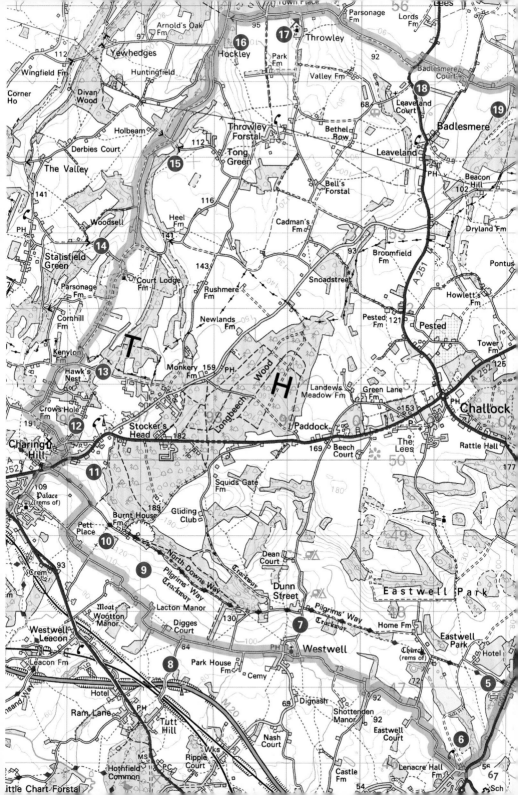

Wooded lanes east of Wye

As mentioned in the previous ride, Wye is a fine centre for cycling, located on the edge of an extensive network of quiet lanes lying within the triangle formed by Canterbury, Ashford and Dover. There is also a good nearby mountain bike ride (see page 106). It is a beautiful wooded area but it is not flat – if you are not climbing a hill you are on your way down one. A little after halfway round the route you may wish to break your journey by visiting the Butterfly Centre at Swingfield Minnis. This is located in MacFarlane's Nurseries and Garden Centre and allows you to walk through a 'tropical rainforest' environment where a whole host of exotic butterflies live amongst bougainvillea, hibiscus, oleander, lantana and gigantic fruiting banana plants. For details and opening times go to www.macfarlanesgardens.co.uk/butterflies.php.
There are many fine pubs dotted along the route and plenty of good views with

perhaps the best left until last: after passing through Hastingleigh you come to a café / restaurant at the top of the Wye Downs overlooking the Low Weald, Romney Marsh and the English Channel. The final descent back down into Wye is the stuff of which dreams are made.

NB In this part of Kent there is an amazingly dense lane network with lots of junctions; this is definitely a ride that is better second and third time round when you know where you are going and don't need to keep consulting the instructions.

Overview
On-road ● 33 miles / 53 kilometres ● Strenuous

Start
Wye, about 4 miles north of Ashford

Parking
Free car park or street parking in Wye

Busy roads
● 200yds on fast, busy B2068 west of Bossingham **8**

● 600yds on A260 south of Denton **17**

Off-road sections
None, although some of the least-used lanes have quite rough tarmac surfaces

Terrain
The hilliest part of Kent - many climbs of 100-200ft (30-60m) and four longer ones

Nearest railway
Wye

Refreshments
Wye
Lots of choice

Sole Street
Compasses Inn
T: 01227 700300

Bossingham
Hop Pocket PH
T: 01227 709866

Barham
Duke of Cumberland PH
T: 01227 831396

Denton
Jackdaw PH
T: 01303 844663

Wootton
Endeavour Inn
T: 01303 844268

Hastingleigh
Bowl Inn
T: 01233 750354

Map pages

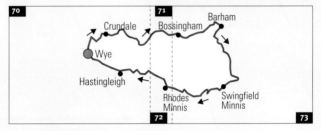

Other rides nearby

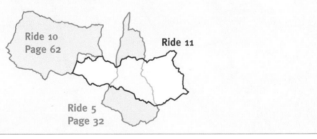

Ride 10
Page 62

Ride 11

Ride 5
Page 32

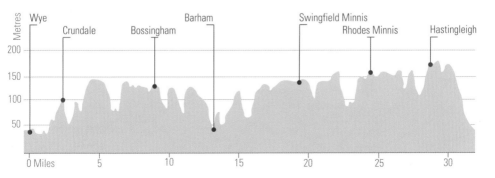

1 With your back to church in Wye turn **L** along High Street then first **L** on Olantigh Road 'Crundale 3'.

2 Shortly after passing Olantigh House on your left, at top of small climb, first **R** (NS) to continue climbing then after ¼ mile first **L** by triangle of grass 'Crundale 1¼'.

3 Long climb, long descent. **Easy to miss:** in village of Crundale, on left-hand bend bear **R** to continue downhill 'Church ¾, Hunt Street 1¼'.

Ride 10 also starts at Wye. Page 62

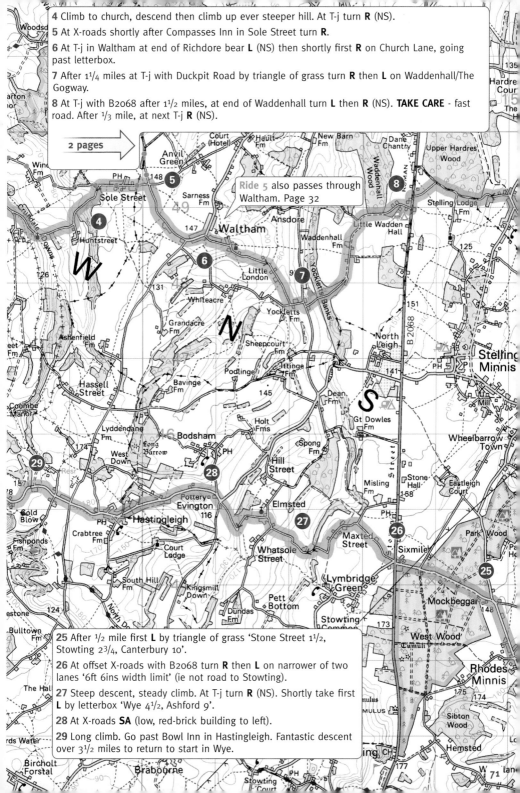

4 Climb to church, descend then climb up ever steeper hill. At T-j turn **R** (NS).

5 At X-roads shortly after Compasses Inn in Sole Street turn **R**.

6 At T-j in Waltham at end of Richdore bear **L** (NS) then shortly first **R** on Church Lane, going past letterbox.

7 After 1¼ miles at T-j with Duckpit Road by triangle of grass turn **R** then **L** on Waddenhall/The Gogway.

8 At T-j with B2068 after 1½ miles, at end of Waddenhall turn **L** then **R** (NS). **TAKE CARE** - fast road. After ⅓ mile, at next T-j **R** (NS).

2 pages →

Ride 5 also passes through Waltham. Page 32

25 After ½ mile first **L** by triangle of grass 'Stone Street 1½, Stowting 2¾, Canterbury 10'.

26 At offset X-roads with B2068 turn **R** then **L** on narrower of two lanes '6ft 6ins width limit' (ie not road to Stowting).

27 Steep descent, steady climb. At T-j turn **R** (NS). Shortly take first **L** by letterbox 'Wye 4½, Ashford 9'.

28 At X-roads **SA** (low, red-brick building to left).

29 Long climb. Go past Bowl Inn in Hastingleigh. Fantastic descent over 3½ miles to return to start in Wye.

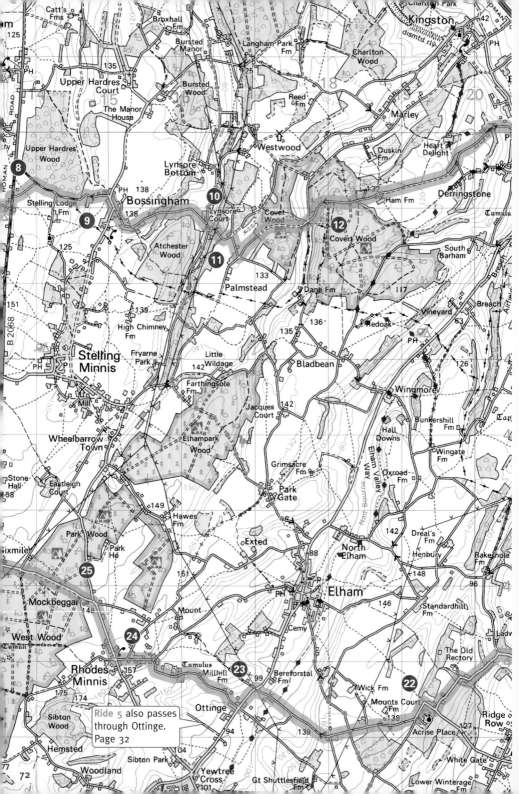

Ride 5 also passes through Ottinge. Page 32

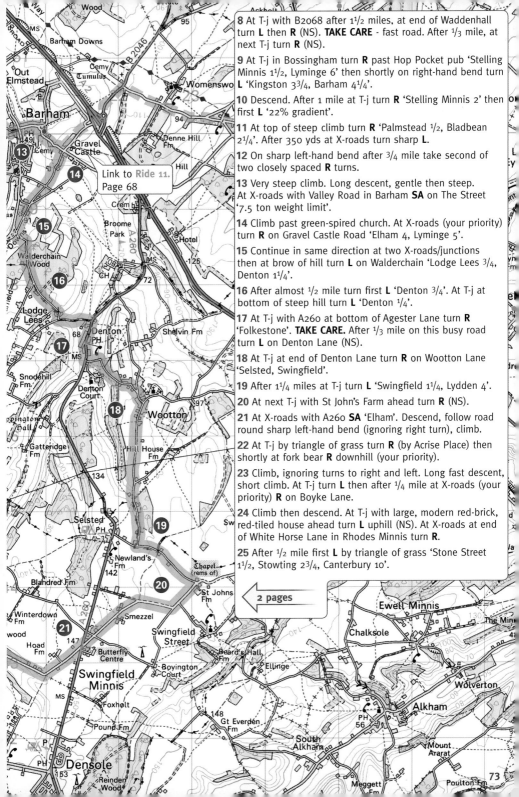

8 At T-j with B2068 after 1½ miles, at end of Waddenhall turn **L** then **R** (NS). **TAKE CARE** - fast road. After ⅓ mile, at next T-j turn **R** (NS).

9 At T-j in Bossingham turn **R** past Hop Pocket pub 'Stelling Minnis 1½, Lyminge 6' then shortly on right-hand bend turn **L** 'Kingston 3¾, Barham 4¼'.

10 Descend. After 1 mile at T-j turn **R** 'Stelling Minnis 2' then first **L** '22% gradient'.

11 At top of steep climb turn **R** 'Palmstead ½, Bladbean 2¼'. After 350 yds at X-roads turn sharp **L**.

12 On sharp left-hand bend after ¾ mile take second of two closely spaced **R** turns.

13 Very steep climb. Long descent, gentle then steep. At X-roads with Valley Road in Barham **SA** on The Street '7.5 ton weight limit'.

14 Climb past green-spired church. At X-roads (your priority) turn **R** on Gravel Castle Road 'Elham 4, Lyminge 5'.

15 Continue in same direction at two X-roads/junctions then at brow of hill turn **L** on Walderchain 'Lodge Lees ¾, Denton 1¼'.

16 After almost ½ mile turn first **L** 'Denton ¾'. At T-j at bottom of steep hill turn **L** 'Denton ¼'.

17 At T-j with A260 at bottom of Agester Lane turn **R** 'Folkestone'. **TAKE CARE.** After ⅓ mile on this busy road turn **L** on Denton Lane (NS).

18 At T-j at end of Denton Lane turn **R** on Wootton Lane 'Selsted, Swingfield'.

19 After 1¼ miles at T-j turn **L** 'Swingfield 1¼, Lydden 4'.

20 At next T-j with St John's Farm ahead turn **R** (NS).

21 At X-roads with A260 **SA** 'Elham'. Descend, follow road round sharp left-hand bend (ignoring right turn), climb.

22 At T-j by triangle of grass turn **R** (by Acrise Place) then shortly at fork bear **R** downhill (your priority).

23 Climb, ignoring turns to right and left. Long fast descent, short climb. At T-j turn **L** then after ¼ mile at X-roads (your priority) **R** on Boyke Lane.

24 Climb then descend. At T-j with large, modern red-brick, red-tiled house ahead turn **L** uphill (NS). At X-roads at end of White Horse Lane in Rhodes Minnis turn **R**.

25 After ½ mile first **L** by triangle of grass 'Stone Street 1½, Stowting 2¾, Canterbury 10'.

Link to **Ride 11.** Page 68

← 2 pages

Hythe & Romney Marsh

The extraordinary landscape of Romney Marsh offers some of the easiest cycling in all of South East England across the pancake-flat countryside bounded by the Royal Military Canal to the north and the English Channel to the south. The land is largely devoted to grazing sheep and making hay for winter feed. Heading west from Hythe the ride leaves town alongside the Royal Military Canal, built in 1804-08 as a defence against the threat of invasion by Napoleonic France. At its

peak there were 1,500 men working on the canal. Its primary function nowadays is to regulate water supply on Romney Marsh, water from the canal being used for irrigation during dry summers and for taking away floodwater in the time of high rainfall. The ride winds its way westwards, parallel with the canal, under huge skies, with the 300ft escarpment delineating the northern horizon. It is suggested you turn around and head back after reaching Ivychurch but it would be easy to explore further west

to Appledore and Rye. There are several more opportunities of refreshments on the return part of the ride, with pubs in Ivychurch, St Mary in the Marsh and Burmarsh, and tearooms just east of here at Lathe Barn. The outward route is rejoined at Botolphs Bridge and followed back into Hythe. If you would like to explore the area further there is a superb traffic-free ride along the promenade running east to Folkestone, signposted as National Cycle Network Route 2.

Overview

On-road ● 26 miles / 42 kilometres ● Easy

Start
Romney, Hythe & Dymchurch
Railway Station in Hythe

Parking
Lots of Pay & Display car parks
in Hythe

Busy roads
None

Off-road sections
One mile outward **1** to **2**
and return **20** on smooth
gravel track alongside the canal

Terrain
Flat!

Nearest railway
Hamstreet

Other rides nearby

Refreshments
Hythe
Lots of choice

Botolphs Bridge
Botolphs Bridge Inn
T: 01303 267346

Ivychurch
Bell Inn
T: 01797 344355

St Mary in the Marsh
Star Inn
T: 01797 362139

Burmarsh
Shepherd & Crook PH
T: 01303 872336

(East of) Burmarsh
Lathe Barn Tearooms
T: 01303 873618

Map pages

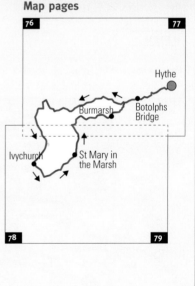

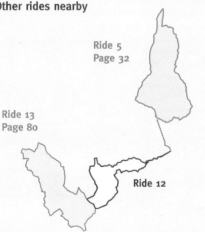

Ride 5
Page 32

Ride 13
Page 80

Ride 12

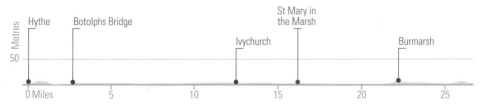

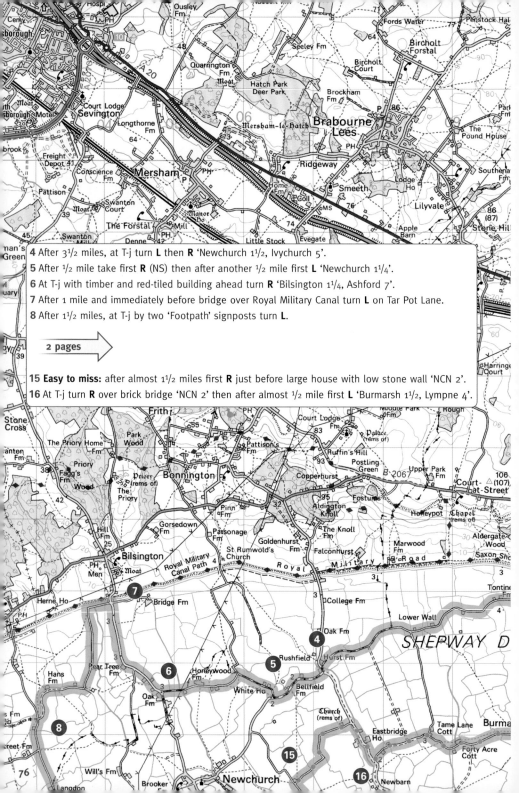

4 After 3½ miles, at T-j turn **L** then **R** 'Newchurch 1½, Ivychurch 5'.

5 After ½ mile take first **R** (NS) then after another ½ mile first **L** 'Newchurch 1¼'.

6 At T-j with timber and red-tiled building ahead turn **R** 'Bilsington 1¼, Ashford 7'.

7 After 1 mile and immediately before bridge over Royal Military Canal turn **L** on Tar Pot Lane.

8 After 1½ miles, at T-j by two 'Footpath' signposts turn **L**.

2 pages →

15 Easy to miss: after almost 1½ miles first **R** just before large house with low stone wall 'NCN 2'.

16 At T-j turn **R** over brick bridge 'NCN 2' then after almost ½ mile first **L** 'Burmarsh 1½, Lympne 4'.

1 With your back to Romney, Hythe & Dymchurch Railway Station in Hythe, turn **L** then **L** again on Green Lane. This turns into wide stone and gravel track parallel to and below canal.

2 After 1 mile bear **L** to cross grey metal bridge over canal then turn **R** on residential road.

3 After 1½ miles at T-j by Botolphs Bridge Inn bear **L** following signs for Newchurch and Aldington.

17 Follow road into Burmarsh then shortly after Shepherd & Crook pub, next **L** on Donkey Street 'Lympne 2½, Hythe 4'.

18 After 1¾ miles at T-j turn **R** 'Lympne 1½, Hythe 3' then immediately after Botolphs Bridge Inn take second of two closely spaced turns to the **R** 'NCN 2' to rejoin outward route.

19 Easy to miss: after 1½ miles keep an eye out for grey metal bridge to cross canal to your **L** (opposite Peregrine Close) 'NCN 2'.

20 Follow this wide smooth gravel track parallel to canal. The track turns to tarmac. At T-j with A259 at end of Green Lane turn **R** to return to start.

Link to Ride 5. Page 32

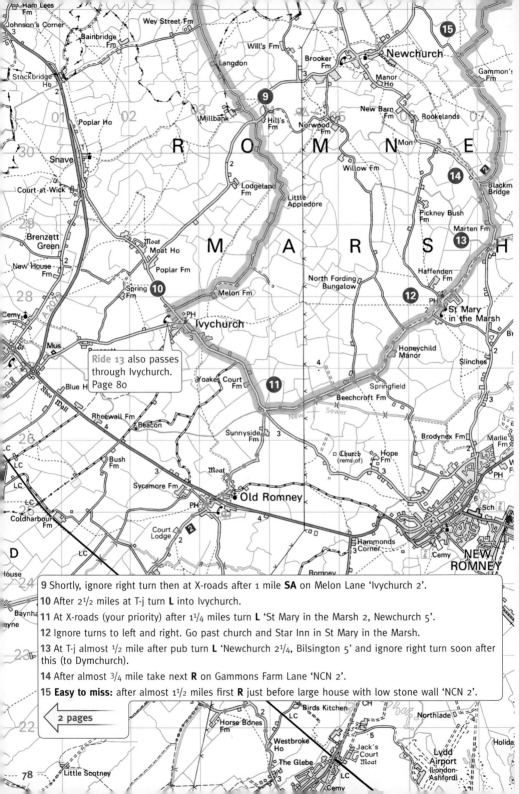

Ride 13 also passes through Ivychurch. Page 80

← 2 pages

9 Shortly, ignore right turn then at X-roads after 1 mile **SA** on Melon Lane 'Ivychurch 2'.

10 After 2½ miles at T-j turn **L** into Ivychurch.

11 At X-roads (your priority) after 1¼ miles turn **L** 'St Mary in the Marsh 2, Newchurch 5'.

12 Ignore turns to left and right. Go past church and Star Inn in St Mary in the Marsh.

13 At T-j almost ½ mile after pub turn **L** 'Newchurch 2¼, Bilsington 5' and ignore right turn soon after this (to Dymchurch).

14 After almost ¾ mile take next **R** on Gammons Farm Lane 'NCN 2'.

15 **Easy to miss:** after almost 1½ miles first **R** just before large house with low stone wall 'NCN 2'.

Appledore & Romney Marsh

This ride and the previous one are the easiest road rides in the book. Much of the time is spent on the lanes criss-crossing Romney Marsh, which is as flat as East Anglian Fenland and looks as though it would be one of the first places to disappear underwater if sea levels rise. Appledore was the scene of an angry demonstration by peasants lead by Wat Tyler in the famous 14th century Peasants' Revolt, protesting against the Poll Tax. The tiny 22ft chapel is all that remains of Horne's Place, a manor house besieged in the uprising. The ride heads north from the village of Appledore with its wide, handsome main street, passes through Appledore Heath and cuts across Shirley Moor on a lane which carries almost no traffic. This contrasts with the only busy section of the ride, about ½ mile on the B2067. The land rises gently through Woodchurch, with its two pubs side by side, to the dizzying heights of 170ft (52m). Before you start suffering from oxygen deprivation the ride turns south through broadleaf woodland and drops back down to Romney Marsh. A meandering course linking Warehorne to Ivychurch, Old Romney and Brookland minimises time on the A259 and A2070, giving you a chance to savour the easiest and flattest roads in all of South East England. For a fuller exploration of Romney Marsh, link this ride to Ride 12 and head east as far as Hythe. You could also ride south to Rye alongside the Military Canal, although this road is busier.

Overview

On-road ● **27 miles / 43 kilometres** ● **Easy**

Start
Appledore, on the B2080 southwest of Ashford

Parking
Free car park at the north end of the village

Busy roads
½ mile on B2067 east of Brook Street ❸

Off-road sections
None

Terrain
Romney Marsh is flat. To the north of the B2067 the land rises gently to 165ft (50m)

Nearest railway
Appledore

Other rides nearby

Refreshments
Appledore
Black Lion PH
T: 01233 758206
Miss Mollett's Tea Room
T: 01233 758555

Woodchurch
Bonny Cravat PH
T: 01233 860345
Six Bells PH
T: 01233 860246

Warehorne
Woolpack Inn
T: 01233 733888

Ivychurch
Bell Inn
T: 01797 344355

Old Romney
Rose & Crown PH
T: 01797 367500

Brookland
Royal Oak PH
T: 01797 344215

Map pages

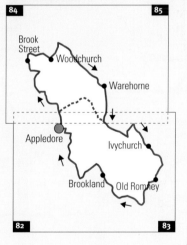

Ride 9
Page 56

Ride 13

Ride 12
Page 74

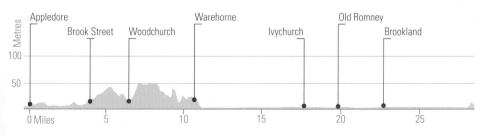

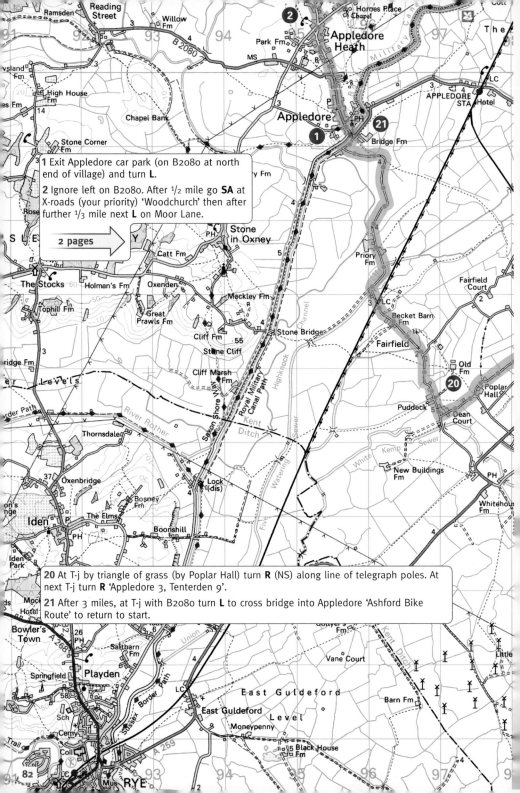

1 Exit Appledore car park (on B2080 at north end of village) and turn **L**.

2 Ignore left on B2080. After ½ mile go **SA** at X-roads (your priority) 'Woodchurch' then after further ⅓ mile next **L** on Moor Lane.

2 pages

20 At T-j by triangle of grass (by Poplar Hall) turn **R** (NS) along line of telegraph poles. At next T-j turn **R** 'Appledore 3, Tenterden 9'.

21 After 3 miles, at T-j with B2080 turn **L** to cross bridge into Appledore 'Ashford Bike Route' to return to start.

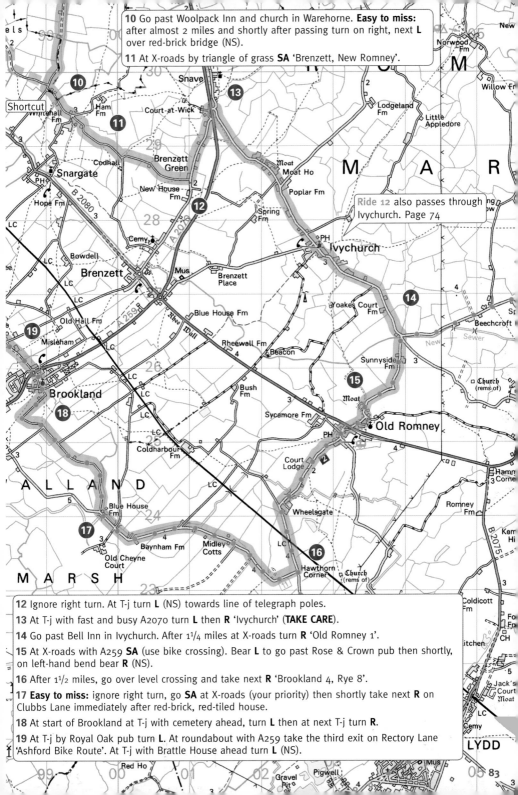

10 Go past Woolpack Inn and church in Warehorne. **Easy to miss:** after almost 2 miles and shortly after passing turn on right, next **L** over red-brick bridge (NS).

11 At X-roads by triangle of grass **SA** 'Brenzett, New Romney'.

Ride **12** also passes through Ivychurch. Page 74

12 Ignore right turn. At T-j turn **L** (NS) towards line of telegraph poles.

13 At T-j with fast and busy A2070 turn **L** then **R** 'Ivychurch' (**TAKE CARE**).

14 Go past Bell Inn in Ivychurch. After 1¼ miles at X-roads turn **R** 'Old Romney 1'.

15 At X-roads with A259 **SA** (use bike crossing). Bear **L** to go past Rose & Crown pub then shortly, on left-hand bend bear **R** (NS).

16 After 1½ miles, go over level crossing and take next **R** 'Brookland 4, Rye 8'.

17 Easy to miss: ignore right turn, go **SA** at X-roads (your priority) then shortly take next **R** on Clubbs Lane immediately after red-brick, red-tiled house.

18 At start of Brookland at T-j with cemetery ahead, turn **L** then at next T-j turn **R**.

19 At T-j by Royal Oak pub turn **L**. At roundabout with A259 take the third exit on Rectory Lane 'Ashford Bike Route'. At T-j with Brattle House ahead turn **L** (NS).

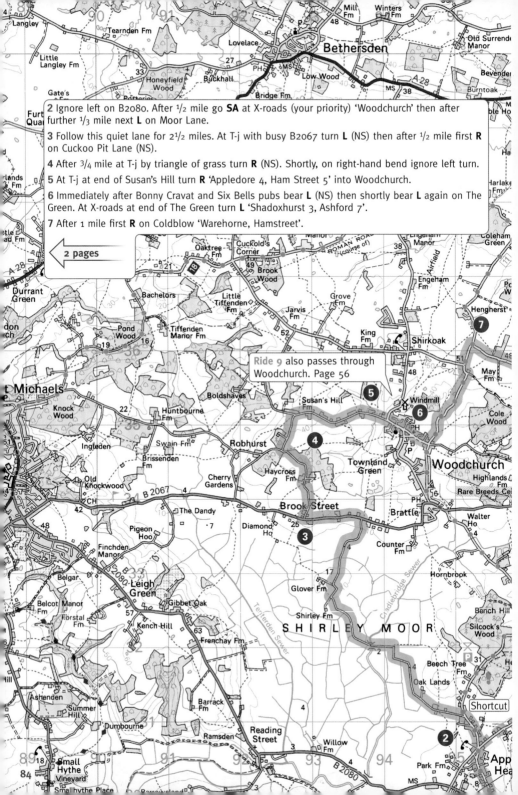

2 Ignore left on B2080. After ½ mile go **SA** at X-roads (your priority) 'Woodchurch' then after further ⅓ mile next **L** on Moor Lane.

3 Follow this quiet lane for 2½ miles. At T-j with busy B2067 turn **L** (NS) then after ½ mile first **R** on Cuckoo Pit Lane (NS).

4 After ¾ mile at T-j by triangle of grass turn **R** (NS). Shortly, on right-hand bend ignore left turn.

5 At T-j at end of Susan's Hill turn **R** 'Appledore 4, Ham Street 5' into Woodchurch.

6 Immediately after Bonny Cravat and Six Bells pubs bear **L** (NS) then shortly bear **L** again on The Green. At X-roads at end of The Green turn **L** 'Shadoxhurst 3, Ashford 7'.

7 After 1 mile first **R** on Coldblow 'Warehorne, Hamstreet'.

2 pages

Ride 9 also passes through Woodchurch. Page 56

Shortcut

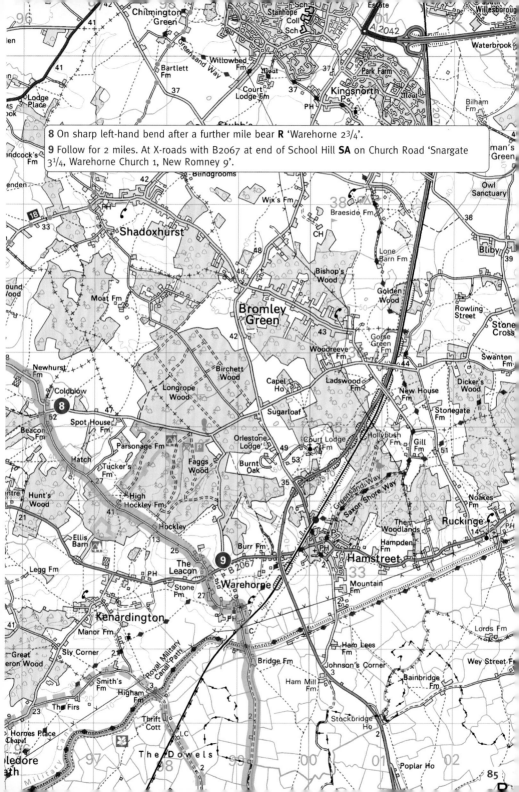

8 On sharp left-hand bend after a further mile bear **R** 'Warehorne 2¾'.

9 Follow for 2 miles. At X-roads with B2067 at end of School Hill **SA** on Church Road 'Snargate 3¼, Warehorne Church 1, New Romney 9'.

Burwash, Brightling & Mayfield

With its three pubs and a tearoom, Burwash is a fine place to look forward to at the end of a ride. You will probably need the refreshment once you have finished as its location on the top of the ridge means that the ride starts with a long descent and ends with a long climb. The descent at the start is fast and furious and is followed by the longest climb of the whole ride; indeed, one of the longest in the whole book (520ft / 159m). At the top you pass close to the obelisk erected by the 19th century Member of Parliament and eccentric, 'Mad Jack' Fuller. He is buried in the churchyard under a 60ft pyramid. Legend has it that he sits in a top hat and tails holding a bottle of claret. South of Woods Corner the ride crosses a series of valleys formed by the small streams heading south from the Weald to the Pevensey Levels. There is a short spell on the Cuckoo Trail at Horam before rejoining the wonderful lane network that enables you to avoid almost entirely the

busier A and B roads. Mayfield is one of the highlights of the trip with its High Street full of attractive buildings. A tiny lane crossing the valley of the infant River Rother links Mayfield back up to the ridge and Burwash. Lying just southwest of Burwash, Bateman's Jacobean mansion was Rudyard Kipling's home from 1902 to 1936. His study, gardens, water mill and one of the first water-driven turbines to produce electricity are all preserved.

Overview

On-road ● **33 miles / 53 kilometres** ● **Moderate / Strenuous**

Start
Free car park in Burwash. The village is on the A265 between Heathfield and Hurst Green (northwest of Hastings)

Parking
The car park is at the west end of Burwash

Busy roads
A265 is used through Burwash (30mph speed limit) **1**

Off-road sections
The Cuckoo Trail (tarmac) is followed for 3/4 mile north of Horam **12** to **13**

Terrain
Hilly with many climbs of 100-200ft (30-60m) and three longer ones

Nearest railway
Stonegate (north of Burwash)

Other rides nearby

Ride 14   Ride 15 Page 92

Refreshments
Burwash
Lots of choice

Woods Corner
Swan Inn
T: 01424 838242

Warbleton
Warbill-in-Tun Inn
T: 01435 830636

Vines Cross
Brewers Arms PH
T: 01435 812288

Horam
Lots of choice

Waldron
Star Inn
T: 01435 812495

Mayfield
Lots of choice

Map pages

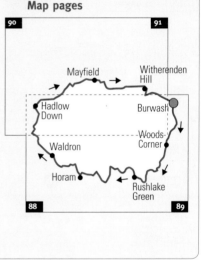

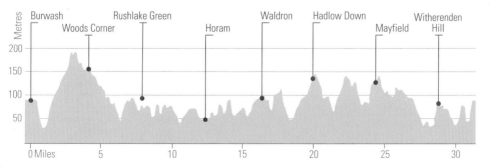

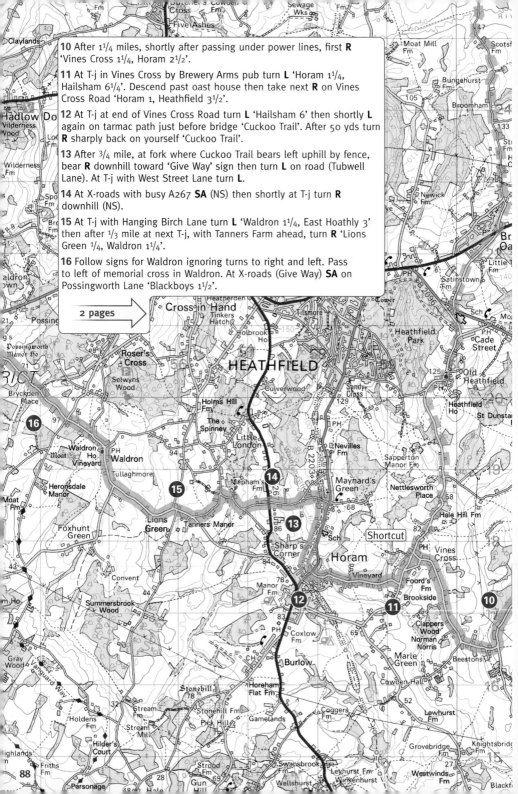

10 After 1¼ miles, shortly after passing under power lines, first **R** 'Vines Cross 1¼, Horam 2½'.

11 At T-j in Vines Cross by Brewery Arms pub turn **L** 'Horam 1¼, Hailsham 6¼'. Descend past oast house then take next **R** on Vines Cross Road 'Horam 1, Heathfield 3½'.

12 At T-j at end of Vines Cross Road turn **L** 'Hailsham 6' then shortly **L** again on tarmac path just before bridge 'Cuckoo Trail'. After 50 yds turn **R** sharply back on yourself 'Cuckoo Trail'.

13 After ¾ mile, at fork where Cuckoo Trail bears left uphill by fence, bear **R** downhill toward 'Give Way' sign then turn **L** on road (Tubwell Lane). At T-j with West Street Lane turn **L**.

14 At X-roads with busy A267 **SA** (NS) then shortly at T-j turn **R** downhill (NS).

15 At T-j with Hanging Birch Lane turn **L** 'Waldron 1¼, East Hoathly 3' then after ⅓ mile at next T-j, with Tanners Farm ahead, turn **R** 'Lions Green ¼, Waldron 1¼'.

16 Follow signs for Waldron ignoring turns to right and left. Pass to left of memorial cross in Waldron. At X-roads (Give Way) **SA** on Possingworth Lane 'Blackboys 1½'.

2 pages →

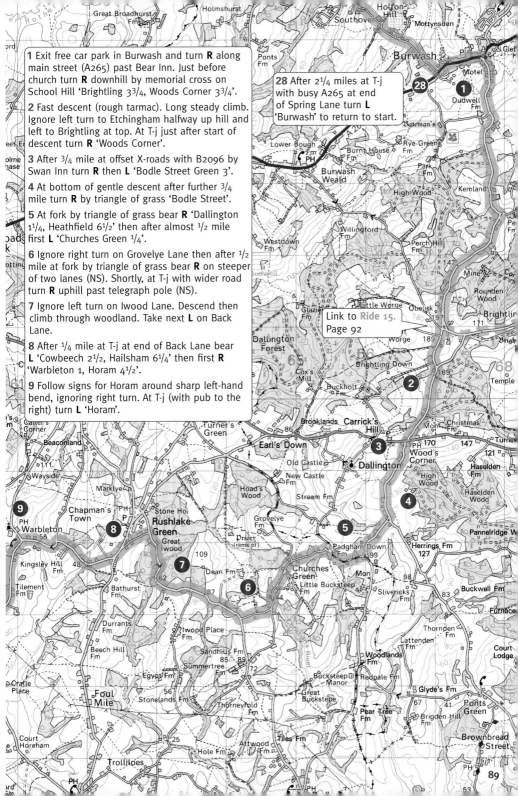

1 Exit free car park in Burwash and turn **R** along main street (A265) past Bear Inn. Just before church turn **R** downhill by memorial cross on School Hill 'Brightling 3³/₄, Woods Corner 3³/₄'.

2 Fast descent (rough tarmac). Long steady climb. Ignore left turn to Etchingham halfway up hill and left to Brightling at top. At T-j just after start of descent turn **R** 'Woods Corner'.

3 After ³/₄ mile at offset X-roads with B2096 by Swan Inn turn **R** then **L** 'Bodle Street Green 3'.

4 At bottom of gentle descent after further ³/₄ mile turn **R** by triangle of grass 'Bodle Street'.

5 At fork by triangle of grass bear **R** 'Dallington 1¹/₄, Heathfield 6¹/₂' then after almost ¹/₂ mile first **L** 'Churches Green ¹/₄'.

6 Ignore right turn on Grovelye Lane then after ¹/₂ mile at fork by triangle of grass bear **R** on steeper of two lanes (NS). Shortly, at T-j with wider road turn **R** uphill past telegraph pole (NS).

7 Ignore left turn on Iwood Lane. Descend then climb through woodland. Take next **L** on Back Lane.

8 After ¹/₄ mile at T-j at end of Back Lane bear **L** 'Cowbeech 2¹/₂, Hailsham 6¹/₄' then first **R** 'Warbleton 1, Horam 4¹/₂'.

9 Follow signs for Horam around sharp left-hand bend, ignoring right turn. At T-j (with pub to the right) turn **L** 'Horam'.

28 After 2¹/₄ miles at T-j with busy A265 at end of Spring Lane turn **L** 'Burwash' to return to start.

Link to **Ride 15.** Page 92

17 At X-roads (with B2102) at end of Possingworth Lane **SA** on Sharlands Lane 'Hadlow Down 2, Buxted 3'.

18 At T-j at end of Sharlands Lane turn **R** then immediately **R** again on Wilderness Lane 'Hadlow Down'. Climb.

19 After 1¾ miles at X-roads with A272 **SA** on School Lane 'Rotherfield 4¼, Crowborough 5' then shortly first **R** on Waghorns Lane 'Rotherfield'.

20 Very easy to miss: after ¼ mile, on fast descent, immediately after sharp right-hand bend, turn **R** on Brick Kiln Lane 'Mayfield'.

21 After 1½ miles, climb past school on Skippers Hill. At X-roads (your priority) **SA** then shortly at T-j with A267 turn **L** then **L** again on Horleigh Green Road 'Rotherfield 3'.

22 Descend, ignore first right. Climb and take next **R** 'Mayfield 1¾'.

23 At T-j with busy A267 **SA** on cobbled path opposite (by metal railings) 'National Cycle Network Route 21' then at T-j with Station Road at top of Fir Toll Close turn **L** to continue uphill 'Mayfield ¼'.

24 On sharp left-hand bend at end of Mayfield High Street bear **R** 'Witherenden 4'. Go past Carpenters Arms then just before Rose & Crown pub bear **R** 'Broad Oak 4, Witherenden 4'.

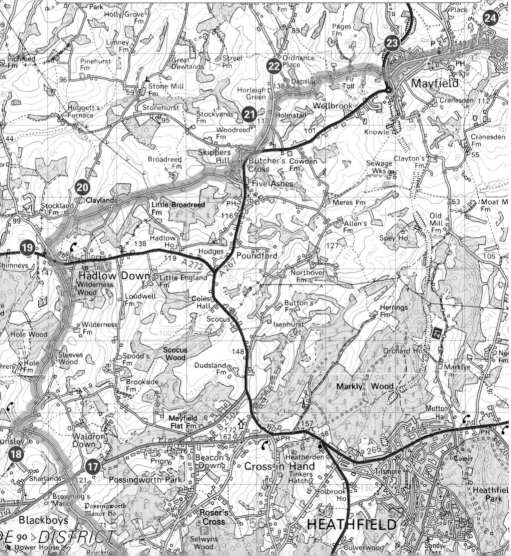

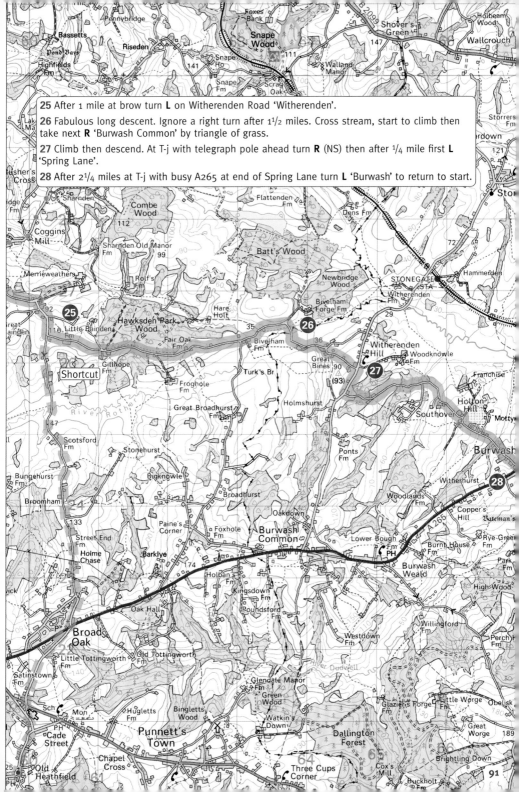

25 After 1 mile at brow turn **L** on Witherenden Road 'Witherenden'.

26 Fabulous long descent. Ignore a right turn after 1½ miles. Cross stream, start to climb then take next **R** 'Burwash Common' by triangle of grass.

27 Climb then descend. At T-j with telegraph pole ahead turn **R** (NS) then after ¼ mile first **L** 'Spring Lane'.

28 After 2¼ miles at T-j with busy A265 at end of Spring Lane turn **L** 'Burwash' to return to start.

Battle, Bodiam, Beckley & Brede

To the east of Ashdown Forest the High Weald divides into three, cut through deeply by the valleys of the River Rother and River Brede. Starting from Battle, scene of the Battle of Hastings, the second half of this ride explores the central outlier of higher land lying between the two rivers. To start the ride you head northwest, climbing from Battle to Netherfield before a rollercoaster down then up to arrive at the highpoint of the trip near to Brightling Church, the burial place of 'Mad Jack' Fuller as described

in the previous ride. A long, gentle descent drops you down into Robertsbridge with its fine main street full of half-timbered houses. The River Rother is crossed twice, first just north of Robertsbridge, then again just after passing Bodiam Castle with its picture-book round corner towers and moat. It was built in 1385 by Sir Edward Dalyngrigge in order to defend the surrounding area from French invasion. However, research shows that the castle was built more for show than as an effective defence: the walls are only 2ft thick and the

moat is relatively shallow and easily drained. The castle was bequeathed to the National Trust in 1926. For information about opening times go to www.nationaltrust.org.uk. Some of the quietest lanes of the day follow Bodiam as you continue east to Beckley then south through wooded hills to Brede. The River Brede itself is not crossed until Whatlington, marking the start of the final climb and setting you up for a fine downhill finish back into Battle.

Overview
On-road ● 33 miles / 53 kilometres ● Moderate

Start
Battle Abbey; Battle is on the A2100 northwest of Hastings

Parking
Lots of Pay & Display car parks in Battle

Busy roads
● A2100 at the start through the centre of Battle **1**

● 600yds on A28 north of Brede **19**

● 400yds on B2244 north of Sedlescombe **21**

Off-road sections
None

Terrain
Hilly with several climbs of 100-200ft (30-60m) and three longer ones

Nearest railway
Battle or Robertsbridge

Refreshments

Battle
Lots of choice

Netherfield
Netherfield Arms PH
T: 01424 838282
White Hart Inn
T: 01424 838382

Robertsbridge
Lots of choice

Salehurst
Salehurst Halt PH
T: 01580 880620

Bodiam (B2244)
Curlew PH
T: 01580 861394

Bodiam
Castle PH
T: 01580 830330

Ewhurst Green
White Dog PH
T: 01580 830264

West of Beckley
Rose & Crown PH
T: 01797 252161

Other rides nearby

Map pages

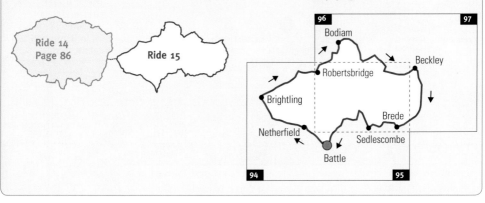

Ride 14
Page 86

Ride 15

96 97
Bodiam
Beckley
Robertsbridge
Brightling
Brede
Netherfield
Sedlescombe
Battle
94 95

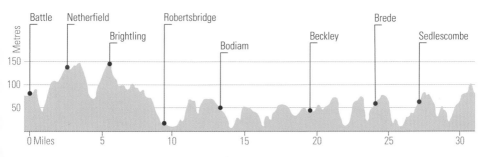

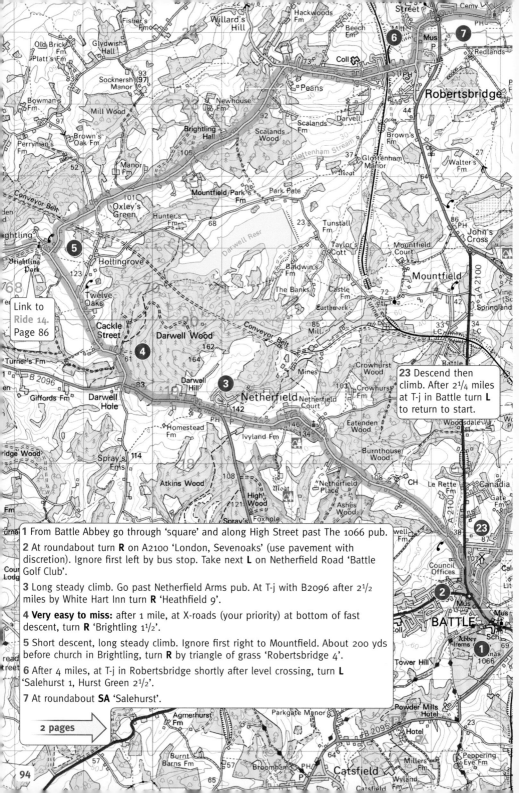

23 Descend then climb. After 2¼ miles at T-j in Battle turn **L** to return to start.

1 From Battle Abbey go through 'square' and along High Street past The 1066 pub.

2 At roundabout turn **R** on A2100 'London, Sevenoaks' (use pavement with discretion). Ignore first left by bus stop. Take next **L** on Netherfield Road 'Battle Golf Club'.

3 Long steady climb. Go past Netherfield Arms pub. At T-j with B2096 after 2½ miles by White Hart Inn turn **R** 'Heathfield 9'.

4 **Very easy to miss:** after 1 mile, at X-roads (your priority) at bottom of fast descent, turn **R** 'Brightling 1½'.

5 Short descent, long steady climb. Ignore first right to Mountfield. About 200 yds before church in Brightling, turn **R** by triangle of grass 'Robertsbridge 4'.

6 After 4 miles, at T-j in Robertsbridge shortly after level crossing, turn **L** 'Salehurst 1, Hurst Green 2½'.

7 At roundabout **SA** 'Salehurst'.

Link to Ride 14. Page 86

2 pages →

19 Descend then climb. At T-j with A28 in Brede at end of Stubb Lane turn **R** then after 1/4 mile first **L** on Pottery Lane 'Narrow Road'.

20 Descend. **Easy to miss:** ignore first right on Frymans Lane and second right to Broad Oak (Reservoir Lane). Take next **R** on Hurst Lane by a red-brick, red-tiled house.

21 At T-j with busy B2244 at end of Hurst Lane turn **L** 'Hastings 7'. **Easy to miss:** after 1/4 mile and just before sharp left-hand bend (with chevrons) turn **R** on narrow 'hidden' lane.

22 At X-roads with A21 **SA** 'Riccards Lane' then shortly at T-j by triangle of grass turn **L** '7.5 ton weight limit'.

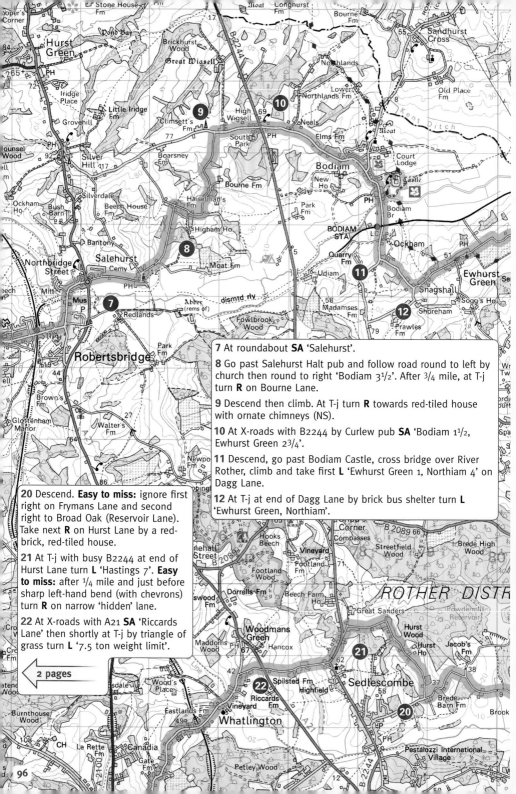

7 At roundabout **SA** 'Salehurst'.

8 Go past Salehurst Halt pub and follow road round to left by church then round to right 'Bodiam 3½'. After ¾ mile, at T-j turn **R** on Bourne Lane.

9 Descend then climb. At T-j turn **R** towards red-tiled house with ornate chimneys (NS).

10 At X-roads with B2244 by Curlew pub **SA** 'Bodiam 1½, Ewhurst Green 2¾'.

11 Descend, go past Bodiam Castle, cross bridge over River Rother, climb and take first **L** 'Ewhurst Green 1, Northiam 4' on Dagg Lane.

12 At T-j at end of Dagg Lane by brick bus shelter turn **L** 'Ewhurst Green, Northiam'.

20 Descend. **Easy to miss:** ignore first right on Frymans Lane and second right to Broad Oak (Reservoir Lane). Take next **R** on Hurst Lane by a red-brick, red-tiled house.

21 At T-j with busy B2244 at end of Hurst Lane turn **L** 'Hastings 7'. **Easy to miss:** after ¼ mile and just before sharp left-hand bend (with chevrons) turn **R** on narrow 'hidden' lane.

22 At X-roads with A21 **SA** 'Riccards Lane' then shortly at T-j by triangle of grass turn **L** '7.5 ton weight limit'.

◀ 2 pages

13 Go past White Dog Inn in Ewhurst Green. **Easy to miss:** after 1½ miles, on sharp left-hand bend turn **R** on Tufton Lane 'Staplecross, Public Road'. Shortly at T-j turn **L** 'Beckley'.

14 After ⅓ mile at fork by triangle of grass bear **R** 'Beckley'. At X-roads with A28 **SA** 'Beckley 1, Rye 7¾'.

15 At T-j with B2165 bear **L** 'Northiam, Rye' then at next T-j (with B2088) turn **R** 'Beckley ¼, Rye 6'.

16 Easy to miss: follow road round to right by memorial cross then on fast descent first **R** on Horseshoe Lane 'Broad Oak 3¾, Udimore 4½'.

17 At X-roads **SA** 'Udimore'.

18 Ignore turns to right and left. After 2½ miles, at T-j with B2089 at top of woodland climb, turn **R** 'Broad Oak 1½, Hastings 10' then first **L** on Stubb Lane.

19 Descend then climb. At T-j with A28 in Brede at end of Stubb Lane turn **R** then after ¼ mile first **L** on Pottery Lane 'Narrow Road'.

Ightham & Mereworth Woods

ghtham is an attractive Kent village with many half-timbered buildings and a couple of good pubs. It is set on the geological divide between the chalk of the North Downs and the sandstone of the High Weald, offering a variety of riding conditions. The route west from the village follows the sandy tracks around Oldbury Hill and Raspit Hill including a set of steps carved into the steep track that leads up to the old Iron Age Hill fort. The meandering woodland tracks contrast with the next part of the ride through orchards, estates and neat countryside around the dramatic old buildings of Ightham Mote and Fairlawne. The third distinctive feature in the ride is the long sweet chestnut coppiced section through Mereworth Woods, a place that has a somewhat primeval feel to it. Another nearby area worth exploring on mountain bikes lies to the east of the village of Wrotham (M20 Jct 2). The North Downs Way, also signposted as the Pilgrims Way, has bridleway or byway status for several miles to the east and you can divert off it to visit

the atmospheric stones of Coldrum Long Barrow. To the west there is another similar ride to this one in the Oxted / Godstone area, described in the companion volume Cycle Tours: *Surrey & West Sussex*.

The largest nearby Forestry Commission holding where you will find some excellent purpose-built singletrack is Bedgebury Forest, about 10 miles southeast of Tunbridge Wells.

Overview

Off-road ● 16 miles / 26 kilometres ● Moderate

Start
Ightham on the A227 / A25 to the east of Sevenoaks

Parking
Free car park at the back of Ightham Village Hall car park on Sevenoaks Road in the centre of the village

Busy roads
Take care at the two crossings of the busy, fast A25

Terrain
Wooded and hilly. Two major climbs:

● 425ft (130m) at the start from Ightham to the top of Raspit Hill **1** to **2**

● 360ft (110m) from Plaxtol to the highpoint in Mereworth Woods **13** to **15**

Nearest railway
Borough Green

Refreshments
Ightham
Chequers Inn
T: 01732 882396
George & Dragon PH
T: 01732 88244

Stone Street
Padwell Arms PH
T: 01732 761532

Plaxtol
Papermarkers Arms PH
T: 01732 810407

B2016/Mereworth Woods
Old Beech Inn
T: 01622 813038

Other rides nearby
For other rides in the area see *South East Mountain Biking – North & South Downs* by Nick Cotton

Map pages

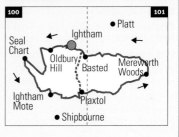

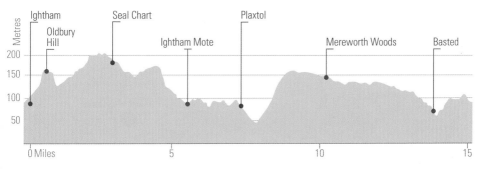

1 Turn **R** out of Ightham village hall car park on Sevenoaks Road. At X-roads with A25 go **SA** (**TAKE CARE**) on Oldbury Lane. Climb past school and continue in same direction as lane becomes no through road. Continue **SA** towards 'No parking, no turning' sign.

2 Pass to **R** of garage on grass 'Bridleway' (on stone marker). Very steep woodland climb with steps. At junction of tracks by 'Oldbury Hill' signboard bear **R** downhill and keep bearing **R**.

3 At T-j with road at bottom of descent turn **L** (by Styants Farm House). At X-roads with A25 turn **L** then **R** 'Bridleway' (**TAKE CARE**).

4 Fine woodland track with sandy sections. At T-j at top of steps turn **R** on track improved with road scrapings. Muddy after rain. Follow in same direction for ½ mile. There are many tracks and forks, several of which rejoin.

5 Emerge at road and bear **R** past school and church. On right-hand bend bear **L** on bridleway leading into woodland. Continue in same direction (again, there are many track junctions).

6 After ½ mile, at T-j with road turn **L** downhill. At T-j with wider road by 'Give Way' sign turn **L** then after 300 yds turn **R** opposite Padwell Arms pub on wide gravel track ('Bridleway' sign is half-hidden in hedge).

7 Pass through orchards. At 5-way junction of roads go **SA** on narrow lane 'Bridleway'. Keep to **R** of orchard then continue in same direction downhill as track narrows and steepens. Follow stream downhill.

8 At T-j with road turn **R**. Follow boundary of Ightham Mote (to your left) then turn sharp **L** between brick pillars (opposite end of red-brick barn of Mote Farm on right) 'Ightham Mote, Bridleway'.

9 Go past Ightham Mote.* At gate at end of enclosed section turn **R** (blue arrow) along field edge. Exit field via bridlegate and turn **L** along wide stone track.

The entrance to Ightham Mote café is through car park on left beyond main house.

10 Go **SA** at busy A227 (**TAKE CARE**) through bridlegate opposite into Fairlawne Estate. At tarmac T-j turn **L** then shortly **R** following 'Bridlepath' signs. Go into field via bridlegate.

11 Follow obvious grass track through estate past magnificent trees. At T-j with road turn **L** then after 300 yds first **R** on The Street.

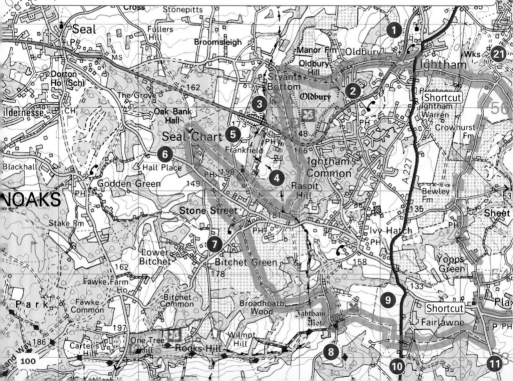

12 Go downhill through Plaxtol past Papermakers Arms pub. Ignore right turn to Dunk Green by telephone box, take next **R** on Brook Lane towards Old Soar Manor.

13 At T-j with Allens Lane turn **L** then as road swings sharp left and becomes Old Soar Road, bear **R** (in effect **SA**) on track (NS). Ignore wide gravel track on right and continue in same direction uphill on a narrower track.

14 Long climb. At T-j with similar track turn **L** uphill. At road junction go **SA** on bridleway opposite. At X-roads with broad track (footpath) go **SA** (blue arrow).

15 Continue in same direction for almost 1¹/₂ miles. At X-roads with fast and busy B2016 go **SA** (Old Beech Inn to your right). **Easy to miss:** after 150 yds, opposite New Pound Lane to the right, turn **L** on narrow track between hedges, beyond metal barrier. Go **SA** at two X-roads of tracks.

16 At next junction, with metal fence to left, as main track swings right, bear **L** (in effect **SA**). After 400 yds keep an eye out for double telegraph pole with metal transformer to left. Turn sharp **L** here on narrow track to go past red-brick Longwall House.

17 Emerge at B2016, turn **R** then **L** after 20 yds, opposite next house, on narrow woodland path 'Bridleway'. Follow obvious earth track. After ¹/₂ mile join wide forest road on U-bend. Bear **R**.

18 After another ¹/₂ mile, shortly after second left-hand bend at bottom of gentle descent, about 20 yds before 'Hurst Wood' sign turn **R** sharply back on yourself by wooden field gate.

19 Go past new executive houses. At junction with The Old Saw Mill turn **L** opposite street sign on narrow track 'Bridleway' (stone marker). At T-j with road turn **L** then **R** on to Crouch Lane towards Borough Green.

20 **Easy to miss:** at bottom of dip, shortly after tarmac drive of Sotts Hole Cottage, turn **L** down steps to join bridleway running parallel with drive. Descend steeply. At road junction by houses turn **L** then **R** on Mill Lane.

21 Climb. At offset X-roads of lanes turn **L** then **R** to cross bridge. At T-j with A227 turn **R** then shortly **L** on Sevenoaks Road to return to Ightham village hall car park.

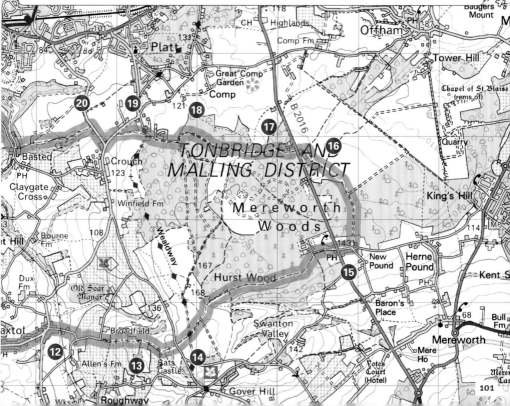

The North Downs Way from Charing to Hollingbourne

U nlike the South Downs Way, which has bridleway status along its whole length from Winchester to Eastbourne, the North Downs Way, running from Farnham to Dover, regularly changes from footpath to bridleway to byway and back again. Mountain bikes are allowed to use byways and bridleways but not footpaths, so it is a rare joy to be able to ride along such a long unbroken stretch of this national trail. It is, in addition, the easiest of the off-road rides in the

book, suitable for novices or even adventurous children. As ever for off-road rides in the southeast, even though some sections have been improved with better drainage, it is recommended doing this ride during the summer and autumn after a few dry days. Undoubtedly the highlight of the ride is the magnificent life-size wooden carving of a resting pilgrim towards the Hollingbourne end of the ride. This is a linear ride so the best option once you have arrived at Hollingbourne is to turn around and retrace your

steps back to Charing. Do not be tempted to use the A20 to complete a circuit: if you want to stick to tarmac for the return route it is best to work out a lane route on the lane network running parallel with the M20 passing through the villages of Harrietsham, Sandway, Lenham Heath, Charing Heath and Coppins Corner. For even easier traffic-free rides nearby it is worth going to Bewl Water or Bedgebury Forest, both of which lie to the southwest of Tunbridge Wells.

Overview

Off-road ● 8¹/₂ miles / 13.7 kilometres one way (17 m / 24.7 km return) ● Easy

Start
Charing, at junction of A252 and A20 northwest of Ashford

Parking
Free car parks in Charing

Busy roads
Take care crossing A252 from Charing to start of North Downs Way ❶

Terrain
The trail rises and falls gently but there are no steep climbs

Nearest railway
Charing or Hollingbourne

Refreshments
Charing
Lots of choice

Hollingbourne
Dirty Habit PH
T: 01622 880880

Other rides nearby
There is also a large Forestry Commission holding at King's Wood, about 5 miles east of Charing. For other rides in the area see *South East Mountain Biking – North & South Downs* by Nick Cotton

Map pages

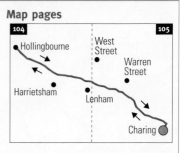

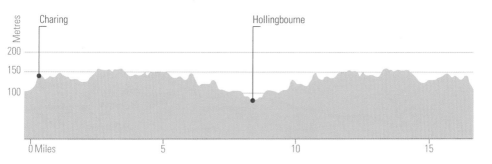

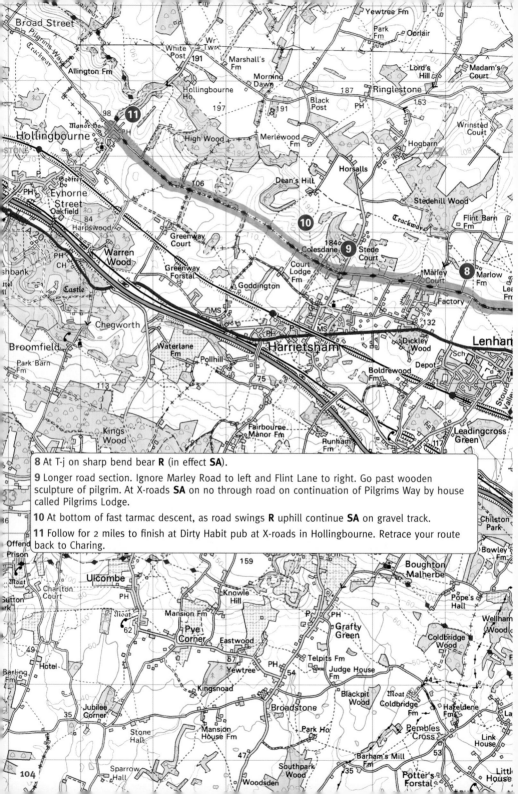

8 At T-j on sharp bend bear **R** (in effect **SA**).

9 Longer road section. Ignore Marley Road to left and Flint Lane to right. Go past wooden sculpture of pilgrim. At X-roads **SA** on no through road on continuation of Pilgrims Way by house called Pilgrims Lodge.

10 At bottom of fast tarmac descent, as road swings **R** uphill continue **SA** on gravel track.

11 Follow for 2 miles to finish at Dirty Habit pub at X-roads in Hollingbourne. Retrace your route back to Charing.

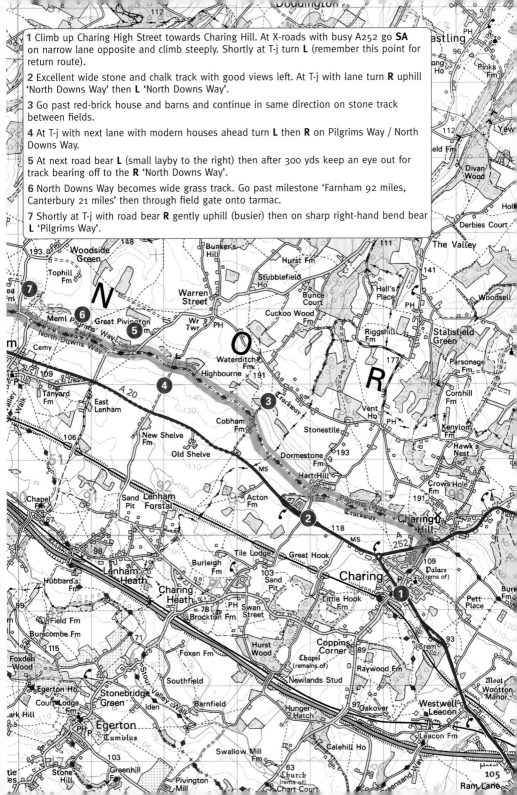

1 Climb up Charing High Street towards Charing Hill. At X-roads with busy A252 go **SA** on narrow lane opposite and climb steeply. Shortly at T-j turn **L** (remember this point for return route).

2 Excellent wide stone and chalk track with good views left. At T-j with lane turn **R** uphill 'North Downs Way' then **L** 'North Downs Way'.

3 Go past red-brick house and barns and continue in same direction on stone track between fields.

4 At T-j with next lane with modern houses ahead turn **L** then **R** on Pilgrims Way / North Downs Way.

5 At next road bear **L** (small layby to the right) then after 300 yds keep an eye out for track bearing off to the **R** 'North Downs Way'.

6 North Downs Way becomes wide grass track. Go past milestone 'Farnham 92 miles, Canterbury 21 miles' then through field gate onto tarmac.

7 Shortly at T-j with road bear **R** gently uphill (busier) then on sharp right-hand bend bear **L** 'Pilgrims Way'.

Wye, the Crundale Downs & King's Wood

Wye is a small, attractive town with several pubs and cafés and it makes a good base for exploring the area by road bike or mountain bike. After a short, gentle climb past the agricultural college you are faced with one of those woodland climbs that you might just make without a dab if you are fit, the conditions are right and you have a slice of luck. Downs and ups come in quick succession before a wonderful ridge section along the Crundale Downs. After passing the Compasses Inn at Sole Street (and one of the few chances of refreshment on the ride) you come across the glue factory, a place you may smell before you see it. A long, gentle woodland descent drops you at the busy A28 and a chance of coffee and cake in the picturesque village of Chilham. The final climb leads up into King's Wood along the North Downs Way, setting you up nicely for the day's best descent off the escarpment back down into the Stour Valley and the return to the start. Just as the triangle formed by Ashford, Dover and Canterbury contains some of Kent's best rides on the lane network, so too this area offers a denser concentration of bridleways than other parts of the county. There is no real substitute for exploring each and every one of them in one direction then the other, at different times of year, to devise the sort of ride that suits you best in terms of distance, difficulty and rideability in all conditions.

Overview

Off-road ● 16 miles / 26 kilometres ● Moderate / Strenuous

Start
Wye, 4 miles northeast
of Ashford

Parking
Free car park or street parking
in Wye

Busy roads
¼ mile on A28 just south of
Chilham 15

Terrain
Wye lies in the valley of the
Great Stour and hills rise up
to the east and west of this:

● 395ft (120m) straight up on
the Wye Downs from the start
1 to 3

● 330ft (100m) from Chilham
up into King's Wood along the
North Downs Way 16 to 18

Nearest railway
Wye

Refreshments
Wye
Lots of choice

Sole Street
Compasses Inn
T: 01227 700300

Chilham
Lots of choice

Other rides nearby
For other rides in the area see
*South East Mountain Biking –
North & South Downs* by Nick
Cotton

Map pages

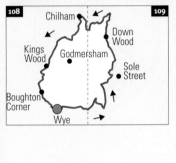

108   Chilham   109
Down Wood
Kings Wood   Godmersham
Sole Street
Boughton Corner
Wye

Metres | Wye   Downs Wood   Chilham   Boughton Corner

King's Wood

200
150
100
50

0 Miles   5   10   15

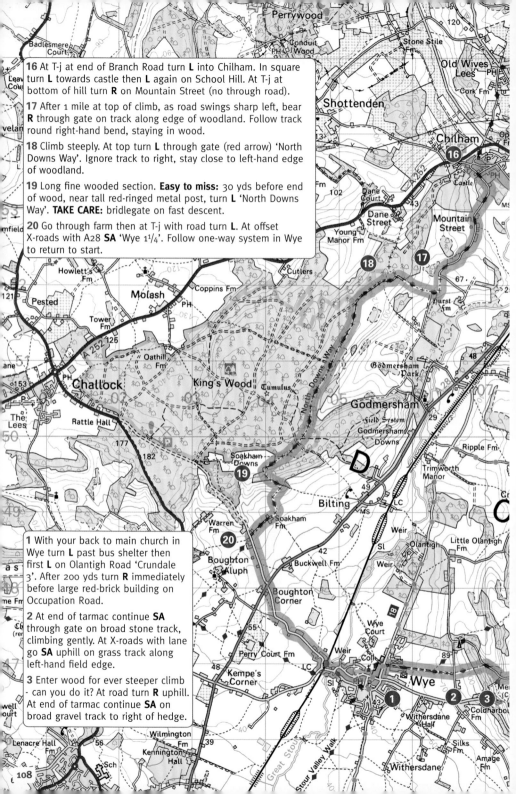

16 At T-j at end of Branch Road turn **L** into Chilham. In square turn **L** towards castle then **L** again on School Hill. At T-j at bottom of hill turn **R** on Mountain Street (no through road).

17 After 1 mile at top of climb, as road swings sharp left, bear **R** through gate on track along edge of woodland. Follow track round right-hand bend, staying in wood.

18 Climb steeply. At top turn **L** through gate (red arrow) 'North Downs Way'. Ignore track to right, stay close to left-hand edge of woodland.

19 Long fine wooded section. **Easy to miss:** 30 yds before end of wood, near tall red-ringed metal post, turn **L** 'North Downs Way'. **TAKE CARE:** bridlegate on fast descent.

20 Go through farm then at T-j with road turn **L**. At offset X-roads with A28 **SA** 'Wye 1¼'. Follow one-way system in Wye to return to start.

1 With your back to main church in Wye turn **L** past bus shelter then first **L** on Olantigh Road 'Crundale 3'. After 200 yds turn **R** immediately before large red-brick building on Occupation Road.

2 At end of tarmac continue **SA** through gate on broad stone track, climbing gently. At X-roads with lane go **SA** uphill on grass track along left-hand field edge.

3 Enter wood for ever steeper climb - can you do it? At road turn **R** uphill. At end of tarmac continue **SA** on broad gravel track to right of hedge.

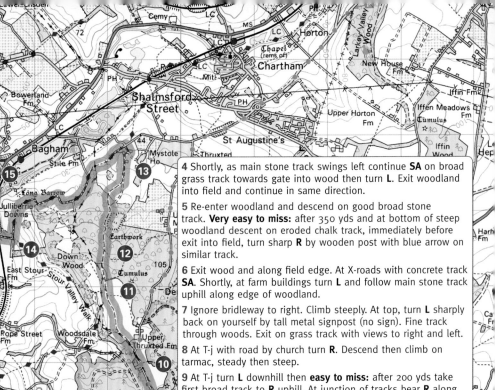

4 Shortly, as main stone track swings left continue **SA** on broad grass track towards gate into wood then turn **L**. Exit woodland into field and continue in same direction.

5 Re-enter woodland and descend on good broad stone track. **Very easy to miss:** after 350 yds and at bottom of steep woodland descent on eroded chalk track, immediately before exit into field, turn sharp **R** by wooden post with blue arrow on similar track.

6 Exit wood and along field edge. At X-roads with concrete track **SA**. Shortly, at farm buildings turn **L** and follow main stone track uphill along edge of woodland.

7 Ignore bridleway to right. Climb steeply. At top, turn **L** sharply back on yourself by tall metal signpost (no sign). Fine track through woods. Exit on grass track with views to right and left.

8 At T-j with road by church turn **R**. Descend then climb on tarmac, steady then steep.

9 At T-j turn **L** downhill then **easy to miss:** after 200 yds take first broad track to **R** uphill. At junction of tracks bear **R** along edge of woodland (may be muddy).

10 At T-j with road with rough car parking area ahead turn **L**. After ½ mile, on right-hand bend shortly after glue factory (it smells!) bear **L** into wood on bridleway waymarked by semi-hidden stone marker (not track alongside fence with red arrow).

11 Exit gate into field and go **SA** between telegraph poles. Go through gate into second field following obvious grassy track between cultivated areas. May be overgrown. At junction of tracks in middle of field by railway sleeper signpost go **SA** towards wood.

12 On reaching wood turn **L** along field edge. Exit field via bridlegate and shortly bear **R**. Gentle descent.

13 Exit wood into field, go **SA** past barns / stables. At tarmac turn **L** then at T-j with road **L** again on gravel track 'Byway, Stour Valley Walk'.

14 **Easy to miss:** follow this track for 1½ miles. Shortly after passing large open field on right, take next **R** downhill on similar track by wooden post with yellow and purple arrows.

15 Cross bridge over railway then 50 yds before busy A28 turn **R** into woodland on track parallel with road. This track runs out and you have to join road for 400 yds. First **L** on Branch Road.

Alfriston & Firle Beacon

This short, but immensely satisfying ride, runs northwest from Alfriston along the base of the South Downs escarpment on its outward leg on a mixture of rough chalk and good gravel tracks. Then, after a steep climb on tarmac up to Firle Beacon, returns on the course of the South Downs Way along the chalk and grass ridge with magnificent views out over the Sussex Weald to the north and the English Channel to the south. Alfriston is a real tourist honeypot full of teashops, restaurants and gift shops. The track along the base of the escarpment has been improved in the past few years with European money as part of a great Anglo-French cycling scheme (www.francobritishcycleplan. org). Firle is a pretty little village with an excellent pub. You may need a bracer to set you up for the steep mile-long road climb that takes you up the face of the South Downs to Firle Beacon at the top. It is certainly worth waiting for a day of good visibility for this ride as the views are potentially stupendous. A word of warning – if it has been raining, take care on the smooth chalk descent back into Alfriston as this can become very slippery when wet. You are certainly not short of tracks to ride around here: in addition to the next ride described, there are singletrack trails in Friston Forest and any number of options south and west of Lewes.

Overview
Off-road ● 11 miles / 18 kilometres ● Moderate (with one steep road climb)

Start
Alfriston, west of Eastbourne

Parking
The Pay & Display car park in Alfriston does not allow you to park for long so it is best to use the wide residential roads to the west of the town – for example, North Road or The Broadway

Busy roads
None

Terrain
The ride follows the base of the South Downs escarpment west from Alfriston to Firle, undulating between 100-230ft (30-70m), then climbs for 615ft (187m) steeply on tarmac then track to follow the ridge back to Alfriston

Nearest railway
Berwick

Refreshments
Alfriston
Lots of choice

Firle
Ram Inn
T: 01273 858222

Other rides nearby
For other rides in the area see *South East Mountain Biking – North & South Downs* by Nick Cotton. The South Downs Way could be followed for many miles to the east or west

Map pages

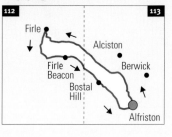

Ride 4

Ride 5
Page 114

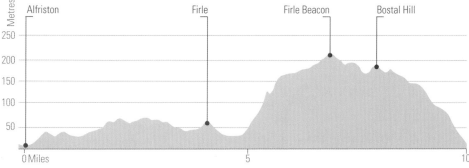

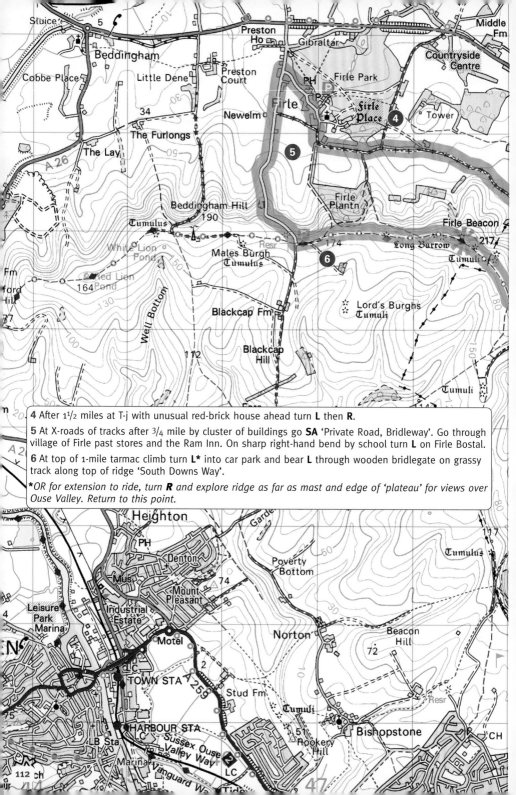

4 After 1½ miles at T-j with unusual red-brick house ahead turn **L** then **R**.

5 At X-roads of tracks after ¾ mile by cluster of buildings go **SA** 'Private Road, Bridleway'. Go through village of Firle past stores and the Ram Inn. On sharp right-hand bend by school turn **L** on Firle Bostal.

6 At top of 1-mile tarmac climb turn **L*** into car park and bear **L** through wooden bridlegate on grassy track along top of ridge 'South Downs Way'.

***OR** for extension to ride, turn **R** and explore ridge as far as mast and edge of 'plateau' for views over Ouse Valley. Return to this point.*

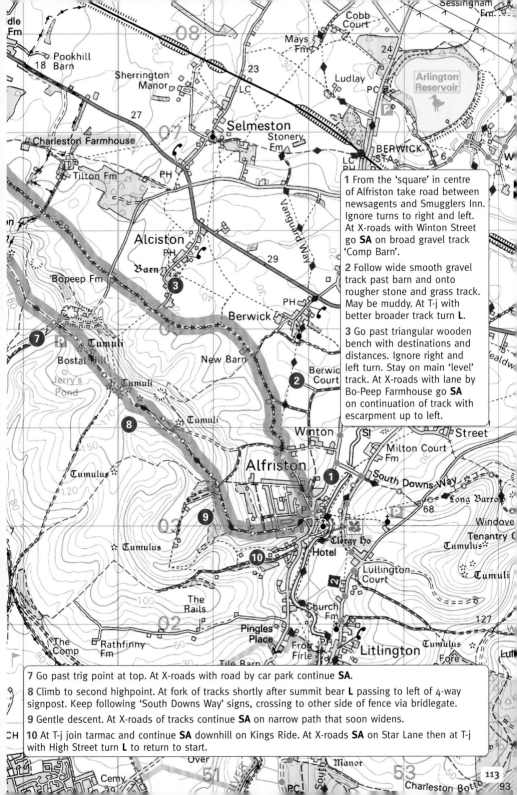

1 From the 'square' in centre of Alfriston take road between newsagents and Smugglers Inn. Ignore turns to right and left. At X-roads with Winton Street go **SA** on broad gravel track 'Comp Barn'.

2 Follow wide smooth gravel track past barn and onto rougher stone and grass track. May be muddy. At T-j with better broader track turn **L**.

3 Go past triangular wooden bench with destinations and distances. Ignore right and left turn. Stay on main 'level' track. At X-roads with lane by Bo-Peep Farmhouse go **SA** on continuation of track with escarpment up to left.

7 Go past trig point at top. At X-roads with road by car park continue **SA**.

8 Climb to second highpoint. At fork of tracks shortly after summit bear **L** passing to left of 4-way signpost. Keep following 'South Downs Way' signs, crossing to other side of fence via bridlegate.

9 Gentle descent. At X-roads of tracks continue **SA** on narrow path that soon widens.

10 At T-j join tarmac and continue **SA** downhill on Kings Ride. At X-roads **SA** on Star Lane then at T-j with High Street turn **L** to return to start.

Alfriston & Friston Forest

This ride explores the final, easternmost section of the South Downs ridge before it plunges down to the sea to finish in Eastbourne. It is a tough ride with four noticeable climbs, rewarded with stunning views in all directions. Leave the honeypot village of Alfriston with its milling tourists and teashops and cross the Cuckmere River, one of only four rivers to cut through the chalk of the South Downs between Winchester and Eastbourne. The first climb is long, but rarely steep, and leads to a viewpoint overlooking Friston Forest to the south and the South Downs across the Cuckmere valley to the west. A fast descent is followed by a short steep climb on Snap Hill. You are now in the heart of Friston Forest and are quite likely to see deer. There are waymarked bike trails in the forest aimed at all levels. Exit the forest and start the long climb up to the top of Willingdon Hill, at first sharply up through fields, then more gently on a broad stone track. The landscape is soft and

rolling with views down into Eastbourne from the brow of the hill. If you like your descents fast and grassy you'll love the drop down towards Jevington. The climb from here through woodland back up on

the Downs is likely to be the muddiest of the ride, but you are soon out of it, on a roof-of-the-world track around the edge of a huge dry valley with a teeth-rattling descent back to Alfriston.

Overview

Off-road ● 14 miles / 23 kilometres ● Strenuous

Start
Alfriston, 6 miles northwest of Eastbourne, off the A27

Parking
The Pay & Display car park in Alfriston does not allow you to park for long so it is best to use the wide residential roads to the west of the town – for example, North Road or Broadway

Busy roads
None

Terrain
This is a tough ride with four main climbs:

● Steady 395ft (120m) climb from the start to Fore Down **2** to **4**

● Steep 200ft (60m) climb on Snap Hill **6**

● Steep then steady 525ft (160m) climb from Friston Forest to the highpoint on Willingdon Hill **12** to **15**

● Final 330ft (100m) climb, steep through woodland then gentle across grass to top of Windover Hill **18** to **20**

Nearest railway
Berwick

Refreshments
Alfriston
Lots of choice

Friston Forest Visitor Centre (just off the route)
Café

Jevington
Eight Bells PH
T: 01323 484442
Jevington Tea Garden
T: 01323 489692

Other rides nearby
The South Downs Way (used for part of this ride) is a long-distance waymarked bridleway running for 100 miles from Winchester to Eastbourne. See also *South East Mountain Biking – North & South Downs* by Nick Cotton

Map pages

Ride 4
Page 110

Ride 5

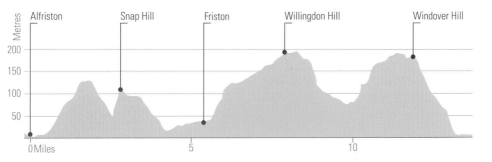

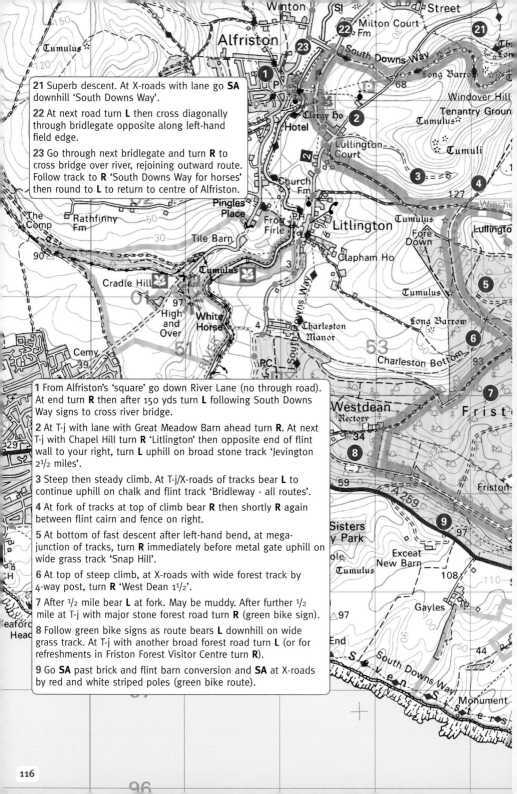

21 Superb descent. At X-roads with lane go **SA** downhill 'South Downs Way'.

22 At next road turn **L** then cross diagonally through bridgelate opposite along left-hand field edge.

23 Go through next bridgelate and turn **R** to cross bridge over river, rejoining outward route. Follow track to **R** 'South Downs Way for horses' then round to **L** to return to centre of Alfriston.

1 From Alfriston's 'square' go down River Lane (no through road). At end turn **R** then after 150 yds turn **L** following South Downs Way signs to cross river bridge.

2 At T-j with lane with Great Meadow Barn ahead turn **R**. At next T-j with Chapel Hill turn **R** 'Litlington' then opposite end of flint wall to your right, turn **L** uphill on broad stone track 'Jevington 2½ miles'.

3 Steep then steady climb. At T-j/X-roads of tracks bear **L** to continue uphill on chalk and flint track 'Bridleway - all routes'.

4 At fork of tracks at top of climb bear **R** then shortly **R** again between flint cairn and fence on right.

5 At bottom of fast descent after left-hand bend, at mega-junction of tracks, turn **R** immediately before metal gate uphill on wide grass track 'Snap Hill'.

6 At top of steep climb, at X-roads with wide forest track by 4-way post, turn **R** 'West Dean 1½'.

7 After ½ mile bear **L** at fork. May be muddy. After further ½ mile at T-j with major stone forest road turn **R** (green bike sign).

8 Follow green bike signs as route bears **L** downhill on wide grass track. At T-j with another broad forest road turn **L** (or for refreshments in Friston Forest Visitor Centre turn **R**).

9 Go **SA** past brick and flint barn conversion and **SA** at X-roads by red and white striped poles (green bike route).

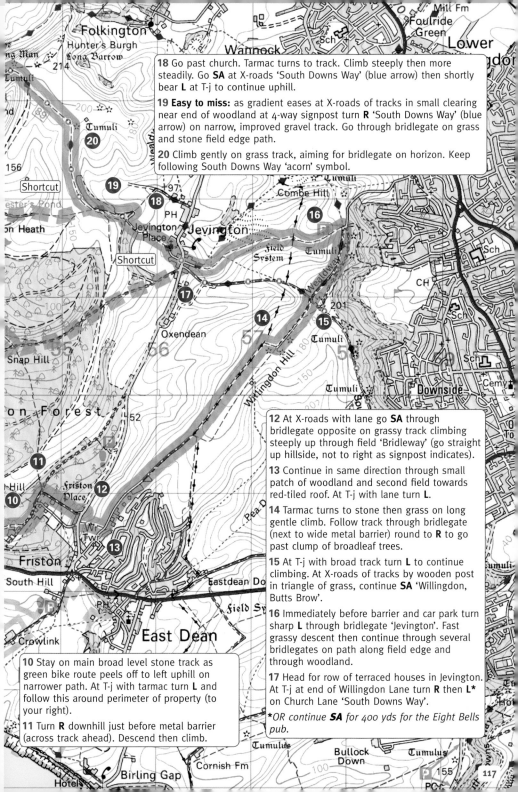

18 Go past church. Tarmac turns to track. Climb steeply then more steadily. Go **SA** at X-roads 'South Downs Way' (blue arrow) then shortly bear **L** at T-j to continue uphill.

19 Easy to miss: as gradient eases at X-roads of tracks in small clearing near end of woodland at 4-way signpost turn **R** 'South Downs Way' (blue arrow) on narrow, improved gravel track. Go through bridlegate on grass and stone field edge path.

20 Climb gently on grass track, aiming for bridlegate on horizon. Keep following South Downs Way 'acorn' symbol.

12 At X-roads with lane go **SA** through bridlegate opposite on grassy track climbing steeply up through field 'Bridleway' (go straight up hillside, not to right as signpost indicates).

13 Continue in same direction through small patch of woodland and second field towards red-tiled roof. At T-j with lane turn **L**.

14 Tarmac turns to stone then grass on long gentle climb. Follow track through bridlegate (next to wide metal barrier) round to **R** to go past clump of broadleaf trees.

15 At T-j with broad track turn **L** to continue climbing. At X-roads of tracks by wooden post in triangle of grass, continue **SA** 'Willingdon, Butts Brow'.

16 Immediately before barrier and car park turn sharp **L** through bridlegate 'Jevington'. Fast grassy descent then continue through several bridlegates on path along field edge and through woodland.

17 Head for row of terraced houses in Jevington. At T-j at end of Willingdon Lane turn **R** then **L*** on Church Lane 'South Downs Way'.

*OR continue **SA** for 400 yds for the Eight Bells pub.*

10 Stay on main broad level stone track as green bike route peels off to left uphill on narrower path. At T-j with tarmac turn **L** and follow this around perimeter of property (to your right).

11 Turn **R** downhill just before metal barrier (across track ahead). Descend then climb.

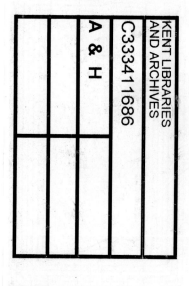